What people are saying about …

ART OF THE MARGINS

D.J. Williams has written a book about freedom—the sort of freedom every author, songwriter, and deep thinker hopes to find, not only in their creative process, but in their life.

Jim Sonefeld, Grammy-Award winning songwriter, author, drummer for Hootie & the Blowfish

Art of the Margins feels like gathering around a bonfire with someone who has journeyed through both beauty and brokenness, discovering creativity and intentionality in the middle of the wilderness. D.J. illustrates how creativity often emerges from the hidden places—the quiet seasons away from the spotlight where wonder fosters deeper artistic expression. This book is honest, inspiring, and brimming with hope for anyone committed to their creative journey.

Tim Timmons, Grammy-nominated singer-songwriter, co-writer of MercyMe's hit "Even If," and founder of 10000 MINUTES

Art of the Margins is more than just a book about channeling one's creativity, and even more than just how God works in the white spaces of our lives. It's a book about eternal purpose—how it is forged in the shadows, the quiet places, the crevices, and the ravines. It's about how, even if no one ever sees, He sees. For every creative soul struggling with purpose, disappointment, disillusionment, ego, and even overconfidence, *Art of the Margins* is for you.

Jaime Jo Wright, bestselling and award-winning author *of The House on Foster Hill* and *The Vanishing at Castle Moreau*

True artistry and spiritual depth are born not from mastery but from a willingness to be shaped by the mysteries we encounter. In *Art* of the Margins, D.J. makes the bold and liberating case that the world "doesn't need more echo chambers—it's desperate for creatives with courage to disrupt." He reminds us that fear and uncertainty are not walls blocking creative expression but can be doorways into it. It's in the tension, the unknown—the margins—that we can discover new depths of creativity and spiritual enrichment. The margins are not places of exile. They're where we stop doing and learn to let the spaces speak.

Brad Hamilton, pastor and author of *When Christians Get It Wrong*

D.J.'s stories are a gift to all of us wandering in the wild, chasing creativity. He invites us to recognize the margins for the gift they are and to create from a place of freedom.

Brian Wells, vice president, member engagement and discipleship, CEO Forum, and author of The League and the Lantern

I expected *Art of the Margins* to remind me how sacred the creative process is and how to navigate the times when that process simply isn't working. This book does that and so much more. The deeply personal stories that D.J. Williams weaves into his perspectives on his life and creative journey are heartbreaking and heroic. Living an authentic, adventurous, and purpose-driven life isn't separate from creating a company, painting a masterpiece, writing a bestseller, or designing an architectural breakthrough; they are intertwined on a single path. This book reminded me that calling is more important than creative success and that creative success can be defined in different ways. But mostly, I loved re-discovering how the barren, lonely, frustrating, and sometimes hopeless place we experience in the margins is critical to the creative process and where the most rewarding breakthroughs happen. Time in the margins is essential to moving us forward to creating with understanding, courage, and purpose.

Andy Lee Johnson, CEO, entrepreneur, inventor, patent holder, and former senior director, creative advertising and production at Walmart

I read *Art of the Margins* on two plane trips. Then I read it again at home. As a full-time freelance producer, composer, arranger, and musician for the past thirty-five years, I connected with it on multiple levels. First, I have so much in common with D.J., having grown up in the same environment and sharing his adventurous spirit. Second, I too have experienced the many ups and downs of the artist's life. Trying to create on a daily basis means wrestling with successes and failures, and this book speaks to that with hope and clarity. I recommend it to any artist in any stage of life.

Paul Langford, producer, composer, and arranger

After years in sports and entertainment, I've learned that what shows up in the spotlight is only a fraction of the story. Art of the Margins captures the deeper reality—that creativity is built in the quiet, unseen work where discipline, resilience, and conviction take root. D.J. Williams offers a grounded, enduring perspective for anyone serious about their craft.

Zane Stoddard, former head of the NBA and NASCAR's Los Angeles entertainment divisions; executive producer of *Logan Lucky*, *NASCAR: The Rise of American Speed*, and *I Am Dale Earnhardt (The Comeback)*

Art of the Margins is a must-read for any creative. D J. Williams is a gifted storyteller who draws from a career spanning music, television, and riveting fiction to illuminate where creativity is forged. His honesty and insight will resonate with anyone who has ever faced the blank canvas, waiting for meaningful inspiration to emerge.

Mitch Kruse, doctor of Religious Studies, author of *Wisdom for the Road*, *Street Smarts from Proverbs*, *Restoration Road*, and former owner, CEO, and auctioneer of Kruse International

ART OF THE MARGINS

Unearthing Your Creativity in Obscurity

D.J. Williams

DAVID C COOK

A MINISTRY OF COOK MEDIA GLOBAL

Every masterpiece begins in the mystery.

Before the brushstroke, before the melody, before the words find rhythm—there is the blank space. It can feel like silence, like solitude, like exile, like riding shotgun in a rusted VW Bug in a third world country alongside a pastor willing to sacrifice himself for the glory of Presence. In the blank space, the wilderness, we stand on the edge of something vast and invisible.

But what if that place isn't a void, an escape, a dead end, but a beginning? What if the absence isn't absence, but anticipation of something deeper in the margins?

You see, beginnings rarely look like center stage. More often, they start in places that feel fragile, exposed, and on the verge of unraveling. For the creative soul, this is sacred ground—a blank canvas, a blank page, an endless wilderness waiting for our creativity. It's more than a metaphor—it's a mirror. Of you. Of me. Of the way Presence is working through us.

Still, most of us crave straight lines and guarantees. The lottery picks for success, instead of the grind of our calling.

We want the GPS; life gives us a dirt road, a busted compass, and a sky that doesn't always tell us north from south. But the soul doesn't thrive on certainty. Our creativity thrives on mystery, on risk, certainty. Our creativity thrives on mystery, on risk, on those holy interruptions when the plan falls apart and we've got no choice but to trust the path beneath our muddied and bloodstained boots. Sometimes it feels like sinking sand, and other times like jagged rocks crashing toward us as an avalanche threatens to end our creativity and our calling.

Deep down we search for the courage to seek the adventure, knowing the journey is less about where it leads and more about who we become along the way. No five year plan, just a first step. We don't need certainty. We need trust. We long for clarity in our calling—He invites us deeper into the margins. The blurry, messy, unfinished spaces of our lives where faith, imagination, and creativity collide in the wild.

The margins are where calling awakens and courage begins. A gift to bravely express our calling through our unique creativity. It's where Presence walks with us to create something eternal through our lives in the mystery, the quiet, the shadows. That's where roots grow. That's where Presence shows up—not in the applause, the spotlight, the accolades—but in the silence between breaths. That's where the mystery begins—and the masterpiece unfolds.

What we discover is the margins are not our enemy, they are an invitation where calling and culture collide with the creative soul. Creativity doesn't arrive with trumpets blaring. It slips in quietly, like a whisper breaking through the slightest noise. Sometimes it finds us in the sanctuary, and other times it appears in a darkened alley, on an overnight flight, or while staring at a blank page with nothing but doubt staring back at us.

Creativity doesn't belong only in galleries, studios, or pulpits. It belongs in the forgotten places around us—in the margins.

ART OF THE MARGINS
Published by David C Cook
4050 Lee Vance Drive
Colorado Springs, CO 80918 U.S.A.

A ministry of Cook Media Global

Integrity Music Limited, a Division of David C Cook
Brighton, East Sussex BN1 2RE, England

Library of Congress Control Number 2026939884
ISBN 978-0-8307-9252-8
eISBN 978-0-8307-9253-5

The Team: Michael Covington, Jeff Gerke, Gina Pottenger, Susan Murdock.
Cover Design: J. R. Schuler
Cover Photo: Robert Merrill

Printed in the United States of America
First Edition 2026
1 2 3 4 5 6 7 8 9 10

061826

AUTHOR'S NOTE

In the wilderness, creatives wander through seasons of uncertainty and obscurity—the margins. Along this journey is where fear is conquered and creativity is forged. Even after all these years, struggles, and breakthroughs, I'm still a wanderer in the wilderness searching for even greater courage toward the edge of brave. I've learned the art of the margins more deeply when those wilderness seasons transformed my craft, my creativity, my calling into holy fire.

I've found a path through the margins to express the creativity burning in my soul. This journey into the wild has redefined success as a creative. If you're daring enough to walk with me toward the edge of brave, to encounter the art of the margins for yourself, then this is an invitation to a great and bold adventure.

But hold on tight—there will be turbulence ... and maybe a few earthquakes.

To the wanderers, the dreamers, the ditch diggers—the doubt killers: This one is for you.

CONTENTS

1

WHERE THE MYSTERY BEGINS

Sweat seeped into my bones as I stepped out from Ninoy Aquino International Airport and inhaled the suffocating humidity. Memories flooded back to me, from being born and raised in Hong Kong until I was fifteen to the times my family visited the Philippines growing up—before we returned to a foreign land, the United States.

As a blue-eyed, brown-haired, expat eight-year-old, I had traveled with my family and fellow missionaries to a village in the Filipino mountains of Davao. Villager residents descended from their tree houses to watch us cross the wooden bridge swaying high above a flowing river. Most had never seen Westerners before, so they marveled at my hairy arms and blue eyes. For one day, I was a celebrity.

Adventures in the Orient are rooted in my DNA.

But years had passed since then, and those adventurous tendencies lay dormant.

Now I was back in a familiar place, stepping into the unknown.

A Filipino pastor greeted me at the curb with a warm smile as locals approached, offering me a better price for a ride to central Manila. After a sixteen-hour flight, I was exhausted yet excited for this new adventure—three weeks on the ground preparing for the arrival of our team to embark on a worship tour across the country.

I wasn't a worship leader. I wasn't a singer. I wasn't even in the band.

But not all creatives stand on a stage in front of the masses.

You see, I was a creative in the margins who lifted up the creatives around me.

My sleepy gaze widened as we approached the pastor's ride. I'm not sure what I expected. A van? A jeepney, maybe. But not an old VW Bug with no windshield. I opened the passenger door and chuckled. Not only was there no windshield, the seats were lawn chairs wedged into place. I tossed my backpack behind the makeshift seats and prayed I'd survive day one.

With a confident smile, the pastor turned the ignition with a screwdriver, and the engine whined to life. Metal rattled all around us with every bump. We pulled into traffic—eight lanes wide, all merging into each other without order or patience. With the open air between us and the taillights ahead, I coughed up a lung as exhaust swept through the Bug like a typhoon. I grasped the side of the door to be sure it wasn't going to swing open. With my other hand, I gripped the lawn chair, certain I was going to fall backward.

Horns blared. Motorbikes and trikes cut through a sea of traffic swerving between lanes. Pedestrians darted across the streets like they were competing in *The Amazing Race*. It was total chaos, yet I loved being in the center of the action.

Between breaths, the moment captured me more than a ride on the Knight Bus in *Harry Potter*. It was a collision of calling, culture, and creativity. Messy. Unpolished. Unpredictable. In the middle of the madness, I caught a glimpse of the mystery and masterpiece, seasons that marked my journey as a creative in the wild.

Every masterpiece begins in the mystery. Before the brushstroke, before the melody, before the words find rhythm—there is the blank space. It can feel like silence, like solitude, like exile ... or like riding shotgun in a rusted VW Bug in a developing country alongside a pastor willing to sacrifice himself for the glory of Presence. In the blank space, the wilderness, we stand on the edge of something vast and invisible.

Yet what if that place isn't a void, an escape, a dead end but a beginning?

What if the absence isn't absence but anticipation of something deeper in the margins?

You see, beginnings rarely look like center stage. More often, they start in places that feel fragile, exposed, and on the verge of unraveling. For the creative soul, this is sacred ground—a blank canvas, a blank page, an endless wilderness waiting for our creativity. It's more than a metaphor: It's a mirror. Of you. Of me. Of the way Presence is working through us.

Still, most of us crave straight lines and guarantees. The lottery picks for success instead of the grind of our calling.

We want the GPS; life gives us a dirt road, a busted compass, and a sky that doesn't always tell us north from south. But the soul doesn't thrive on certainty. Our creativity thrives on mystery, on risk, on those holy interruptions when the plan falls apart and we've got no choice but to trust the path beneath our muddied and bloodstained boots. Sometimes it feels like sinking sand, and other times like jagged rocks crashing toward us as an avalanche threatens to end our creativity and our calling.

Deep down, we search for the courage to seek the adventure, knowing the journey is less about where it leads and more about who we become along the way. No five-year plan; just a first step. We don't need certainty. We need trust. We long for clarity in our calling—He invites us deeper into the margins. The blurry, messy, unfinished spaces of our lives where faith, imagination, and creativity collide in the wild.

The margins are where calling awakens and courage begins. A gift to bravely express our calling through our unique creativity. It's where Presence walks with us to create something eternal through our lives in the mystery, the quiet, the shadows. That's where roots grow. That's where Presence shows up—not in the applause, the spotlight, or the accolades, but in the silence between breaths. That's where the mystery begins and the masterpiece unfolds.

What we discover is that the margins are not our enemy: They are an invitation to where calling and culture collide with the creative soul. Creativity doesn't arrive with trumpets blaring. It slips in quietly, like a whisper breaking through the slightest noise. Sometimes it finds us in the sanctuary, and other times it appears in the darkest days, or while staring at a blank page with nothing but doubt staring back at us.

Most want the story to begin in the spotlight: on the stage, with applause, where everyone nods and affirms we've made it. But what if the greater calling is found in the margins, in the wilderness seasons? More often, our lives begin in obscurity where there's no reward in sight, when all we have offers a flicker of hope that maybe, just maybe, Presence has placed creativity within us and it's worth bringing to life.

Creativity doesn't belong only in galleries, studios, or pulpits.

It belongs in the forgotten places around us—in the margins.

My journey of creativity and faith hasn't been a straight line or filled with guaranteed spotlights. Between breaths, Presence has invited me into the mystery, risk, and sacrifice. Oftentimes kicking and other times cursing before surrender. Countless prayers offered over the years, many answered and others still whispered in the wilderness. Each time a path narrows in the margins, I'm tempted to stop and pray forever instead of stepping into what's next with unrelenting courage. As the years have passed, I'm more aware of the cost to be in His presence.

Deep down, I believe we're hungry to encounter His masterpiece.

No GPS needed. No compass necessary. Only the margins will bring us there.

The first glimpses of my creativity weren't polished. They were messy. Scribbled lines on a page that no one would ever read. Half-formed ideas as an entrepreneur to build a record company within a church to reach the world. Most of it seemed impossible. Yet an invitation from Presence kept pulling me back into the margins, and it still does today. A sense that the margins—the overlooked, the unseen, the forgotten places—might be the very ground where creativity takes root and the masterpiece from Presence is revealed.

After accepting the invitation and landing in Manila, I had a sense that I was still wandering aimlessly in the wilderness. I wasn't on center stage. I wasn't delivering a message to a packed house. To many, I wasn't even on the page. But I was sweating through every piece of clothing as creativity ignited in my spirit. And that's the mystery. Presence seems to delight in starting His greatest work far from the spotlight. You see, creativity isn't born in comfort; it's birthed in the tension of being unseen yet still choosing to create.

I'd left my corporate career behind and taken one of the biggest risks of my life, one that had landed me in the streets and barrios of the Philippines. No guarantees. No real idea of where this journey would one day lead. No clear path. Unnoticed by others. Just my boots on the ground, carrying me through the margins one step at a time.

Looking back, I'm reminded of the sacrifices required to risk in the mystery. Sometimes the only way forward is to surrender the past and future, to leave the illusion of control behind. Each time, Presence has picked me up from my knees and helped me walk again, even when I didn't know how much farther I could go.

Maybe that's where you are now. No clear path. Unnoticed by others. Uncertain. You're questioning whether your voice matters—whether your creativity matters. You're wondering if the effort is worth the sacrifice when no one applauds. That's where the mystery begins. That's where calling takes shape. And that's where the margins, as overlooked as they may feel, become sacred ground.

As a fellow wanderer, I encourage you to keep walking. Even when the edges of life close in. Especially when the edges of life close in. Because grace and creativity are found in the detours, the late nights, the impossibles, the hard yeses, and the brave noes. That's the beautiful tension of the margins: You don't control the journey, but you can choose whether to take the next brave step. Light or heavy. Free or fearful. And if you lean into the journey, you just might discover that the detour was the destination of creativity all along.

Every story is birthed in the ordinary. Before the call, before the risk, before the transformation—there is obscurity. That's where the soil of creativity is tilled.

David was the boy who would be king. But I don't picture him in royal robes. I see him in the fields, alone, tending sheep with only the sky for an audience. No crowds. Just obscurity, responsibility, writing songs no one heard.

That's where his story began. Not in a palace. Not on the battlefield. But in the margins.

Bezalel and Oholiab weren't household names written on the scorecard of biblical heroes. They were artisans tucked into Exodus (see Ex. 31, 35–38), filled with the Spirit to craft a tabernacle that would carry Presence. Imagine having a calling no one else could see. Hidden in Scripture, their creativity shaped a dwelling place for the divine. Their creativity reveals that the margins are not just preparation—they are the very place Presence chooses to reveal His glory through us.

Even Jesus didn't begin His ministry on a grand stage. He spent decades in Nazareth, living quietly before a three-year epic journey to the cross. The greatest story ever told began in obscurity ... and changed the course of eternal history.

The margins are not simply a blank space; they are proving grounds for calling. They strip away pretense and teach us what remains when the applause is absent. Zechariah reminds us:

> Do not despise these small beginnings, for the LORD rejoices to see the work begin. (Zech. 4:10 NLT)

Creativity thrives here because it's not forced to perform. It doesn't have to justify itself by results. It can simply exist, breathe, stumble, and grow. We are reminded in these seasons how our worth comes from a closeness to Presence, who called us when we were unnoticed. You see, creativity isn't about the applause—it's about an invitation. It's not only about inspiration—it's about resilience. It's the bridge between our calling and a culture desperate for authenticity.

Every story begins in obscurity: in mission fields, mailrooms, workshops, home offices, dorm rooms, corner suites, forgotten places. That's where the first steps are taken. Small, hidden, unseen. Yet those genesis moments are never wasted, because they carry seeds of transformation.

If we are to encounter a bold, creative soul rooted in sacrifice, these beginnings require an end to complacency. We cannot simply stand still as religious statues in our calling. We cannot despise the silence or the small start. Instead, we must lean into it. Walk it out. And trust that what feels ordinary today may one day be revealed as the sacred ground where our stories truly began.

Much like that VW Bug ride in Manila—chaotic, risky, unpolished—beginnings may not look like much. But don't mistake disorder, disarray, or disruption for insignificance. Presence rejoices in the start, however fragile or messy it feels. We may not be wearing a robe in a palace, but we're tiptoeing onto the battlefield.

A battle cry to the courageous resounds, reverberates, and reignites us to see what the world overlooks and to discover that the greatest works of Presence often begin in the shadows. Step away from the pressure of performance, visibility, and hustle, and return to the place where the most powerful and authentic creativity is born ... through the art of the margins.

Maybe you're an artist wrestling with self-doubt. Maybe you're an entrepreneur diligently building what no one else understands. Maybe you're a leader navigating the culture while trying to remain faithful to a deeper call. You're on a sacred collision with creativity, calling, and culture. There are no formulas or hacks, and yet you're searching for a light that shines on the blank spaces in the wilderness where masterpieces are formed, where purpose is refined, and where Presence whispers loudest.

Because in the end, the margins aren't a detour from your purpose. They're the wild, unlit path where your story begins to unfold. Where every brushstroke in the dark, every sentence written in silence, every note played in devotion, and every risk chosen without applause is woven into the narrative Presence is writing through you. The margins are not the end of the story. They're the genesis where the truest stories are born.

My earnest prayer is that when you turn the page, Presence will meet you where you are—whether you're disillusioned, burned out, full of questions, or fully immersed in the creative flow, inspired, and building something bold. Let this moment be a reminder that the creative process—messy or masterful, hidden or seen—is sacred.

Your work still matters. Your voice still carries weight. And whether you're wrestling in the dark or soaring in the light, you are embarking on a bold adventure beyond your wildest imagination. If you're battling doubt in the deafening silence or skyrocketing from a breakthrough, your story isn't over. The brush is still in the hand of Presence. You were never meant to fit the mold. Your creativity was meant to be forged courageously in the margins, to shape your unique expression for an eternal purpose.

And this is only the beginning.

Step deeper into those blank spaces to uncover what the art of the margins can reveal about creativity, calling, culture, and the courage to take the next brave step.

Keep creating. Keep believing.

Because what begins in the margins can reshape the world.

2

BURIED DOESN'T MEAN DEAD

A hand reached down and pressed a palm into the dirt as silence hung heavily, surrounded by pitch blackness. Fingers curled into the soil still damp from the rain. The earth looked lifeless, cold, even forgotten. Nothing stirred, no sign of beauty. To anyone passing by, it would seem like nothing memorable. Just another patch of dirt. But beneath the surface, unseen and uncelebrated, a seed had been planted.

Hidden in the dark. Waiting.

You thought you'd buried the seed—the dream, the idea, the story, the spark that once made your heart pound with excitement. Maybe it slipped beneath the surface because life got loud. Maybe it was discarded in disappointment. Maybe it scattered as you chased someone else's dream and left the seed behind. Maybe it simply disappeared, and you're convinced it wasn't meant to grow.

But Presence doesn't throw dreams away. He conceals them until His perfect time. He shows us how burial and planting look the same on the outside. We see delay; He sees depth. We see disappointment; He's growing maturity. We see silence; He's strengthening the roots. And He's just getting started.

The creative life isn't a straight line. It spirals. It circles back. It digs a few more ditches. It resurrects. And sometimes the most powerful works we'll ever create are the ones that needed to be hidden for a season so they could rise with even more clarity, conviction, discipline, and courage. That's why we don't dig up old dreams for nostalgia's sake. In the margins, we recognize what Presence planted in us wasn't forgotten—it was protected.

After surviving my ride in the VW Bug through the polluted streets and barrios of Manila, I returned to the States and dedicated nearly a decade of creativity to growing a worship ministry while building an indie record label from the ground up. Our pace was relentless, and the fruit of our efforts was humbling. Praises echoed beyond the walls of our church. Songs were embraced. Record deals were struck. A movement was born. Influential leaders visited our community, then invited us to lead worship in their communities too.

Navigating a worship ministry and the business of Christian music was its own minefield, but we found our way for a season. Songs written and produced, as well as the records sold, reached places we never imagined. From the forgotten of this world to megacities throughout Asia to the open fields of Africa to the jungles of South America to churches, arenas, stadiums, and coliseums in the United States.

Opportunities seemed to mirror significance in calling.

But I hadn't yet spent seasons in the margins to recognize the difference.

What began in a small office grew to capturing moments that carried hope to the world. We witnessed followers encouraged and seekers welcomed in surrender to Presence. Each of us brought our unique creativity to the cause as we traveled across continents to proclaim the message and share stories of the forgotten. We witnessed lives changed, and the miraculous unfolded before us.

> But you have God-blessed eyes—eyes that see! And God-blessed ears—ears that hear! A lot of people, prophets and humble believers among them, would have given anything to see what you are seeing, to hear what you are hearing, but never had a chance. (Matt. 13:16–17)

It was a privilege. It was exhilarating. It was exhausting.

In many ways, it became my identity. A prayer whispered years earlier was answered. And yet the sacrifices came with a heavy cost. Beneath the surface, the mission that once gave me life was draining me. My dedication pressed ahead, ignoring a stirring in my soul. But the strain on my calling left me questioning whether this was where I belonged.

Years grinding in the work left me running on empty. A constant demand to sacrifice more, to push harder, to accept decisions out of my control, and to embrace the vision of others left me asking hard questions. Perhaps the greatest challenge to serving in community is choosing whether to lay down one's calling to serve the calling of another. Maybe we're afraid that if we sacrifice for others, then we won't encounter all that Presence has for us.

What if sacrifice is the root of our creativity?

I questioned my purpose. I challenged my faith. A faith I'd been raised in since I was eight years old. I'd watched the toll and aftermath of ministry, and there was a sense my world was shifting. *Is this still where Presence wants me? Is this all there is to my creativity? Is my calling forever, or is this just one season?*

Ministry had once been pure joy, but now a heaviness lingered. The songs and the mission were still powerful, but the rhythm of the ministry was out of sync. And I was afraid of surrendering in the margins, because that meant losing what was built and walking away from a decade of blood, sweat, and sacrifice. Oftentimes we're quick to encourage others to surrender all of themselves to Presence ... while we keep a vise grip on our calling.

In many ways, it felt like a burial.

Those raised in the church are familiar with the story of Lazarus. When he died, everyone believed his story was over. Four days later, Jesus arrived. Imagine the wonders Lazarus experienced in the heavenly realms before he was raised from the dead. But Jesus resurrected him back to this world in a new life. In the same way, I never expected dead dreams to be brought back to life as I wrestled with burying this season.

I wouldn't only be leaving behind a career. I was also burying a calling and all that it required. I was returning an invitation granted years earlier by Presence. Honestly, I wasn't sure I had the courage to risk it all again. Even in my doubt, I was already stepping deeper into the margins.

A worship tour in Zambia ended in a field where tens of thousands of Zambians worshipped each night. Weeks earlier, we'd been in Singapore when we received word that a record label had decided to back out of an agreed-upon deal for a live record. We were on our own. I wanted to force the label to follow through with their commitments, but as many are aware, oftentimes that's not how it plays out in ministry. Accountability isn't always black and white. We scrambled to carve out the extra resources, since we were already committed—which included budgets for recording a live record *and* filming a documentary.

The last city on the tour was also one of the roughest in Zambia. Not only did we have to build the stage from scratch each night, we also had to tear down all the equipment, instruments, and audio gear before leaving, or else there would be nothing left at daybreak. Each morning, we returned, started over, and set up again—praying the constant power surges and outages wouldn't blow up our gear.

Most of our team spent their days visiting church leaders, outreaches, and orphanages. A small crew stayed behind with me in the sweltering heat racing against the clock to be ready for the next night's concert. Each evening, our team led onstage alongside hundreds of choir members from churches across the city, singing and dancing, as a sea of humanity who worshipped in the open field were shadowed in the dark.

All the while, beneath the stage my crew crawled from one post to the next, hammering splintered pieces together so the stage wouldn't collapse. We even chased thieves who attempted to break into our bus and steal our belongings. And we kept our sights on the first-timers who stood in the crowds, those who had never been on a mission trip before.

This was full-contact creativity.

And it demanded courage amidst the chaos.

Cameras rolled during those weeks—except for when I stood face-to-face with the owner of the sound company, who attempted to shake us down for an extra ten grand. Not to mention the corruption we encountered with local leaders, evident when we first arrived and discovered nothing was in place like it was supposed to be.

None of that made it into the final cut.

At the end of each night, I stepped onto the stage sweaty, filthy, and frustrated as our team snapped selfies with the choir and crowds after a powerful night lifting up the praises of Presence. We were on the front lines, each in our own way.

After the final night, our team returned to the States with stories to tell. I stayed behind with several others for a last-minute excursion to the Zambezi River. Three days to recover and film B-roll for the documentary seemed like a great idea. Now, I'm a city boy, so I had no clue what I was signing up for ... until we arrived at an airfield and boarded a four-seater aircraft. Less than an hour later, I gazed out the window as zebras and giraffes crossed the open plains below. It was breathtaking.

We landed on a dirt strip of road in the middle of nowhere. On the ground, we were careful not to step in the welcome piles of elephant dung. Let's just say I'm glad we landed during daylight. We walked toward a waiting Land Rover, and it hit me: No power. No cell service. No internet. No communication.

We were unplugged, and adventure awaited us.

We reached camp on the shores of the Zambezi River, and each chose a tent of our own. It wasn't until nightfall, as growls and roars echoed in the distance, that I realized I was an idiot for staying in a tent by myself.

After a restless night, I rolled off the cot and watched a troop of baboons race through our camp. Of course, the mosquito netting on the tent wasn't going to stop an animal from tearing me to shreds. Fortunately, my hairy arms and legs camouflaged me from being prey.

We set out on a fishing boat along the river, and cameras rolled. Hippos sauntered along the shore. Elephants eyed us from the cliffs. I thought I'd connect with our guide, so I asked him if he'd ever heard the names of any celebrities. His response was a blank stare. We were in another world.

Before noon, we returned to camp and climbed into the Land Rover before heading straight into the bush. On this part of our safari, we captured footage of impalas and zebras. Nice and easy. But within the hour, we had followed a trail deep into the bush where we came within fifty feet of an elephant with giant ivory tusks.

Our guide was seated behind the wheel, describing where we were as I rolled camera. Then he said the words I will never forget: "We can get closer."

My missionary-kid spidey senses tingled as I attempted to explain how the camera had a great zoom feature. But the Land Rover was already rolling forward. My heartbeat quickened. For a split second, I believed we were safe. Then a resounding trumpeting sound shattered the peacefulness. The elephant's ears flared, and his stare locked in on us. We weren't at the circus; we were out in the wild. As the elephant charged, I kept rolling, mainly for the simple fact that if I died, at least everyone would know how it happened.

The guide shifted in reverse and punched the accelerator, launching us backward at breakneck speed. Holy words were spoken. Confession: None of them were "Holy Spirit." As the elephant gained ground, narrowing the distance to ten feet, the guide suddenly slammed on the brakes, stood up in his seat, and waved his arms.

Dust swept through the air as the camera rolled. To my amazement, the elephant stopped less than five feet from the Land Rover. My heart skipped a few beats, then pounded even harder. No one moved. Seconds ticked. The elephant just stared at us, and we stared at him. After a few minutes, the incredible beast casually turned his head and sauntered away between the trees as if nothing had happened.

Still, the camera rolled.

When we returned to camp and played the footage for the other guides, their nervous laughter and raised brows were enough proof of how close we'd come to wrestling an African wonder.

Later that afternoon, I stood near the shore as hippos dove into the water. I replayed my encounter with the elephant and realized it was a wake-up call. Presence slammed on the brakes, stood in His seat, and waved His hands to get my attention. He wanted me to turn my gaze back toward Him instead of my circumstance.

As a vibrant sunset swept over the jungle, I heard a gentle whisper in my spirit: "You're going to write about this place one day." Presence was reminding me, "What you thought was buried isn't gone. It's waiting." My season was shifting in the margins. Presence was planting something new in the wild—a dream I'd had since I was young: to be a storyteller.

The creativity I thought I'd lost was beginning to grow beneath the soil. Even though I didn't know when my current season in ministry would end, this moment was a creative resurrection. Presence's idea was greater than my disappointment.

You see, dormant dreams still carry life.

Moses spent forty years in exile, hidden in Midian. The calling that once burned in him to deliver his people seemed finished. He was a shepherd now, not a leader. Yet his time in the desert wasn't wasted—it was preparation. And when the bush caught fire, the buried calling resurfaced with a blaze that couldn't be ignored.

Fanny Crosby was blind from infancy. To many, her life was limited. Hidden. Buried. Yet she wrote more than eight thousand hymns with more than one hundred million copies printed—songs sung by generations of believers. "Blessed assurance, Jesus is mine! O, what a foretaste of glory divine."[1] She couldn't see with her eyes, but her soul poured out with clarity. She tapped into a vision that grows only in the dark. Her blindness didn't prevent her creativity; it propelled it. The very challenge the world thought disqualified her became the soil of her songs.

Imagine a woman huddled in a corner café in Edinburgh, her baby stroller pushed against the wall. She's scribbling words into a notebook. The world sees a single mother, but what they don't see is a story rising from the ashes of uncertainty. In the midst of the silence, J. K. Rowling's words carried life. She had no publisher, no audience, no reason to keep writing other than a determination that the story inside her mattered. Day after day, she returned to the page. The notebooks piled up, hidden from the world, buried in obscurity.

Until one day, those words surfaced.

What began in the margins became a global phenomenon.

For one of my favorite authors, a buried dream was only dormant.

On the shores of the Zambezi, I was living a similar experience in my own way. When the stories in my soul came to life—half-buried manuscripts, scribbles in journals, ideas locked away—each one came with more depth, more urgency, more conviction than if I had written them years before. The delay wasn't wasted space. It was seeds of creativity planted deep in the soil. And when the time was right, the buried dream resurrected where the Zambezi wound through the wilderness.

In the margins, the creative life spirals, circles back, *and* resurrects. It's not linear. It rarely runs in predictable lines. It faces off with giant beasts in the wild. It interrupts life and pulls us out of the ordinary into the unknown.

For Moses, it was the flaming bush. For Fanny Crosby, it was blindness turned into melodies. For J. K. Rowling, it was a delayed train and corner cafés. For me, it was three days on the Zambezi. For you, it may be a whisper in the night, a tug you can't ignore, a dream you thought buried but still beats in your soul. Remember, burial and planting may look the same, but only planting carries resurrection. What you thought was buried and gone may actually be Presence's way of saying, "Not yet."

> Unless a kernel of wheat falls to the ground and dies, it remains only a single seed. But if it dies, it produces many seeds. (John 12:24 NIV)

Just because your creativity is underground doesn't mean it's over. Growth is still happening.

Like Lazarus, Presence can raise those dreams from the dead ... in the margins.

As I look back, I see now how leaving this season of ministry wasn't the end—it was the burial of a seed to encounter new life. The years of sacrifice weren't wasted; they were watering. The Zambezi River was a reminder that Presence doesn't discard dreams. He plants them. And what we bury—dreams we believe are dormant—He resurrects in His time.

The question is, Will we trust Him in the silence long enough for the roots to grow?

3

WEIGHT OF WINNING

The van rattled out of Lusaka, Zambia, its windows streaked with dust, carrying us deeper into the bush. Beside me sat a woman named Stella, her steely stare fixed on the horizon. She carried herself with broad shoulders and a steadied presence. She wasn't weighed down with the pursuit of achievement or anxious about what might come next. She lived surrendered—faithful to the work in front of her on this day.

When the van finally slowed at a small village near Mungule, children spilled from the doorway of a cinder-block structure. More faces framed the openings where windows should've been. Laughter and excitement rose across this desolate village. I swallowed hard as the children's smiles broke me with the innocence of their youth.

Stella was the first to move as we gathered in a circle while the villagers joined us. She lifted a sixty-pound bag of food onto her shoulder as though it were the most natural act of worship. No lights. No stage. No instruments. No audience. Just obedience.

Not wanting to be the weaker one, I bent to grab another bag. I breathed deep and powered through as the weight dug into my shoulders. My muscles burned with the pressure I carried, yet the burden of repeating past wins, of proving I still had something left in the tank, weighed even heavier. But with each step through the village, I caught a glimpse of how creativity in the margins wasn't about winning. It was about carrying the weight of what mattered most.

From one mud-and-straw hut to the next, the distribution of food began. Our team worked together in the blazing heat. Stella asked several of us to follow her deeper into the bush. There were families too weak and sick to come, so we took the supplies to them. For hours, we hiked through the tall yellow grass, flowing streams, thick mud, and heavy brush. Each step carried unfiltered worship without a single note sung—Presence using us in our own creativity to show His love to those who could give nothing in return.

In a clearing, a mother waited, clutching her daughter. Consumed by fever, the young girl's body hung limp in her mother's arms. My heart sank. The food we carried could not heal her. Medicine was nowhere within miles. Frustration and fear surged. I wanted to do more, to fix it. But I was powerless.

I looked to Stella. Her faith never wavered. She simply asked us to pray. As her voice rose, strong and steady, we placed the girl in the hands of Presence. Surrendering. When the prayer ended, I opened my eyes to see the girl staring straight at me. For one long moment, everything stilled as life breathed into this child. No more words. Just the undeniable, miraculous, healing power of Presence in the margins where we had nothing left to give.

Walking back to the village, I was speechless. And for those who know me, that might be the greatest miracle of all. Stella led the way, unshaken, her love and belief relentless. She knew what mattered most—surrendering as an offering to meet the needs in the name of Presence. There will never be a spotlight on Stella's story. No applause or accolades. But I'm convinced heaven knows her name. And now you do too.

Next, we traveled to Livingstone and experienced one of the great wonders of the world: Victoria Falls. As I stared at this magnificent sight, the lessons of the village remained. Presence and Creativity—names of God who are one and the same—expressed His mighty power in the roaring waterfalls and in the gentle touch of a young girl on the edge of the other side. He reminded me that heroes of the faith rarely stand on stages or trend in headlines. More often, they walk dirt paths the world forgets, courageous and brave, alongside the thunderous power of Presence.

When I returned to Zambia less than a year later for the worship tour and found myself standing on the shores of the Zambezi, I thought about Stella. The village had offered me a glimpse of how faithfulness, servanthood, prayer, and love mark the wanderers of Presence and Creativity. Maybe I could experience this same kind of faith when I returned home. I held on to the gentle whisper that drifted across the waters of the Zambezi inspired by heroes like Stella.

Of course, I kept the charging-elephant footage locked in the archives and the young girl who was healed as a memory in my heart. My creative roots were growing deeper beneath the soil. In the margins, I was challenged not to live in my past success. Instead, the art of the margins was beginning to resurrect fresh creativity to out-trust my fear in the present. Still, I was stepping further into a wilderness season, unsure of how long the silence would last.

Within months after returning from Zambia, an unexpected opportunity presented itself: an offer to become the GM/COO of an entertainment company in Los Angeles. My calling wasn't over; it was resurrected and sprouting in a fresh season. In many ways, witnessing Stella's courage offered me the same bravery to step into the unknown, strong and steady.

Naturally, there would be opinions and rumors. But I was a creative in the shadows, away from the spotlight. I was the one no one remembered. On the outside looking in, the ministry was successful—whatever that means in the church world. (Even now, I question whether our definition of success and influence aligns with the calling of Presence. But that's another wilderness path for another time.)

As expected, the questions fired. Why are you leaving? Is it for more money? Is it because of a disagreement? Is there a rift within the ranks? I sought counsel from several trusted friends and answered those questions privately for myself. Our conversations only confirmed what I already knew to be true: The margins were nudging me to take an even greater risk.

For some, the decision was hard to understand. Others didn't know I was gone until months later. And yes, rumors about me leaving for more money swirled. Naturally. More money is the default explanation, while the truth is oftentimes much deeper. But the transition was in motion. In a matter of weeks, I walked into a corner office of the entertainment company a few blocks from the Warner Bros. studio lot. As if having wandered for years in a dark cave and finding an opening on the other side, a new journey in the wild began.

Strangely, next door to our suite was the *Extreme Makeover* production offices. Maybe it was a sign to remind me who was in control. What I had experienced in the margins leading up to this season offered me enough courage to trust that Presence would do an extreme makeover in my creativity, in my calling, and in my life.

Right or wrong, the years of serving and sacrifice in vocational ministry were left in the rearview. Rumors faded. My phone stopped ringing. Everyone moved on. Interesting how quickly that happens. Strange how community is oftentimes rooted in what we have to offer rather than simply being and growing together. When the dust settled, what remained were lifelong friendships and my calling as a creative who was willing to go deeper in trusting the art of the margins.

I stepped boldly into this season surrounded by a diverse community. Some well-known. Some seasoned in the industry. Others up-and-coming, with creative dreams of their own. From a rock band to a pop artist to a reggae songwriter to a future film director to a leader from a global brand. Some of it was like central casting, and some of it was a band of misfits. I chose to embrace the challenge and bring my A game. At the same time, I tried to leave the wins of the past where they belonged.

Within months, we were in discussions and negotiations with record labels, studios, and television networks. Budgets. Staff. Marketing. Promotion. Studio sessions. Rehearsals. Music videos. Touring. All of these creative expressions happened at the same time. We were the underdogs, and we had a lot to prove. Looking back on this season, the lessons gained and the relationships made during my time there infused in me a fresh perspective about creativity, friendship, and the lure of success, as the company charged toward a joint venture with Interscope Geffen A&M Records.

The village. Stella. The girl. Victoria Falls. The Zambezi. Those moments brought me to this unexpected place. But what was Presence showing me about success? Success can be a spotlight ... or a silent burden. As a creative, nothing is more paralyzing than the pressure to outdo ourselves. And nothing is more devastating than falling from the mountaintop.

Songs that reached the charts—and the ones that bombed. Shows renewed for another season—and the ones that were canceled. Films that garnered a standing ovation—and the ones critics blasted. Books that hit the bestseller list—and the ones left on the bottom of the pile. Brand launches that changed everything—and the ones left on the verge of bankruptcy. Deals that skyrocketed a start-up—and the ones that tore partners apart.

The higher we rise, the more we risk, the greater the weight of success.

The lower we fall, the less we believe, the more our failures leave us stuck in the past.

But in the margins, we have to choose to walk in freedom from those chains.

Imagine if a church leader sought greater influence by purchasing pallets of books, then hid them in storage rooms on campus. Why? So their book could be labeled a *New York Times* bestseller and they could receive all the perks that come with notoriety. Imagine a record company altering sales reports so its artists could climb the charts, all in the name of Presence. When we compromise the greater good because of our need for success, our souls are chained. The art of the margins teaches us that the weight of winning is not at all costs.

How far are we willing to go for success? How much are we willing to compromise for notoriety? Will we leave others behind in the name of our calling? Do we want to live free from those chains, or are we willing to carry this silent burden?

When we chase our own success rather than the freedom of creativity engrained in our souls, there's a shift in the margins. What once flowed from passion now drips with pressure and compromise. We're no longer chasing beauty in rhythms, melodies, words, frames of light, ideas, innovations, dreams; we're avoiding failure or fictionalizing success.

We're no longer free—we're performing. We're no longer trusting—we're controlling. We're no longer creating—we're competing. And oftentimes we're compromising with ourselves ... and with Presence.

One moment, we're lost in the joy of creativity's flow. The next, we're checking the charts, the streams, the reviews, the competition, the score, the trends. Our creativity shifts to conform for clicks, views, endorsements, accolades, ratings, or the next deal. All the while, we're walking a tightwire of compromise. We start creating, not to discover beauty but to defend flaws. We stop creating to explore when success is the endgame, because success can be a double-edged blade. So we have to guard our hearts from the chains of compromise.

Success needs to rise higher. Creativity longs to go deeper. On our knees before our Creator. There is no compromise. And there is no comparison.

Comparison is a thief with a thousand disguises. Sometimes it shows up as envy. Sometimes it snaps back as insecurity. Sometimes it rages as jealousy. Sometimes it exiles as inferiority. Sometimes it gloats as perfectionism. But more often, comparison is a silent burden that seeps beneath the soil as we compete against our former selves—when we achieved success.

Is this song more powerful than the last? Did this episode capture the story more deeply? Was my last book the best in the series? Did the message resonate stronger than before? Was the viral response a reflection of a better product? Did people love this launch more than the previous one?

We replay old victories and losses as if they are final verdicts. We measure today's offering against yesterday's applause. But our calling was never about comparison or our definition of success. Our worth doesn't hang in the balance of what the world applauds, unless the applause is resounding toward Presence.

In the margins, we can be free from both the weight of success and the burden of failure. We're not called to outperform our past; we're called to out-trust our fear. Every other burden—expectation, reputation, perception, acceptance, approval—was never meant to be carried by us.

When we create from compromise, we're left empty. When we create from comparison, we're chained. Success and winning become an anchor pulling us to the depths of the sea. But in the margins, the true weight is found. The only weight we're meant to carry: wonder.

When we create from wonder, there is freedom. The only win that matters is obedience. When we create from obedience, there is strength. Envy becomes gratitude. Jealousy becomes trust. Inferiority becomes confidence. Perfectionism becomes grace. Past victories or losses no longer chain us in future caves in the wild. Conformity no longer shapes our calling. Pride no longer distorts our visions. Formulas no longer restrict our creativity.

The question isn't, Will this be as good as last time?

The question is, What am I called to create now?

In the margins, Presence isn't calling us to repeat greatness; He's calling us to reveal truth. When the silence lingers, stillness exposes whether we are creating for the crowd or the One who called us. Success and failure drain the soul, but surrender anchors the heart. We chase certainty and get chaos. We chase compromise and are left empty. We chase comparison and are chained in discontent. But when we embrace surrender, we find freedom and peace in our calling.

Surrendering in the margins guides us to a renewed kind of success. While wonder offers us freedom and obedience provides strength, surrender roots our creativity in Presence. As creatives in the margins, we can't use up surrender. The more we give, the more of Him we receive.

Success is no longer measured in numbers, awards, influence, or fame. Instead, winning in the margins is surrendering in obedience, faith, love, joy, peace, patience, kindness, goodness, faithfulness, gentleness, and self-control. The world says: Win at all costs. Presence says: Walk with Me. The world says: Greatness demands compromise. Presence says: Reveal My truth. The world says: You are in control of your own life. Presence says: Lift up your eyes.

> As for me, may I never boast about anything except the cross of our Lord Jesus Christ. Because of that cross, my interest in this world has been crucified, and the world's interest in me has also died. (Gal. 6:14 NLT)

In the margins, we test our work not against others nor against our past but against the call Presence has given us today. Not yesterday. Not tomorrow. Today. There is a simplicity of courage rooted in obedience and surrender. A bravery in surrendering ourselves, our creativity, our craft in obscurity. That's the blank space, the blank page, where the art of the margins teaches us to boast about Presence and nothing more.

> I have been crucified with Christ and I no longer live, but Christ lives in me. The life I now live in the body, I live by faith in the Son of God, who loved me and gave himself for me. (Gal. 2:20 NIV).

Success in the world and in culture may open doors, but neither will sustain in the margins; only the beauty of our calling can. Obedience expressed through our lives and creativity chases beauty. We go deeper. We fall on our knees in surrender. We refuse to compromise. We resist comparison. We face the darkness head-on with courage and resilience. And we breathe in wonder and exhale freedom.

That is the weight of winning.

4

LIGHT IN THE WILD

An endless desert stretched across a starry night. Thousands of weary travelers traversing a vast wilderness. No map. No city walls. Only the unknown. Children cried as mothers whispered urgently. Men eyed the shadows, fearful and on edge. An enemy hunted them with an army of thousands, weapons, chariots, and a deadly pharaoh.

Then it appeared: a pillar of fire blazing in an ink-filled sky. A magnificent light shimmering against a barren landscape. It wasn't just a flame; it was a presence. A promise. Proof they were not abandoned in the wild.

Every step forward was illuminated by flame lighting an unknown path to keep evil at bay. Moses carried a righteous staff. The Israelites faced an impassable sea. One powerful Presence provided for their needs in the margins. A reminder even the harshest wilderness fails to hide the light.

That's what the wild does: It strips away the familiar, the comfortable, the controllable. In the emptiness, Presence burns brighter than anything we can carry ourselves.

The wilderness doesn't announce itself. Sometimes it looks like obscurity, feels like failure, or seems like the aftermath of success. Other times, it looks like life. The wilderness sweeps through as seasons when the path we thought defined our calling shifts. A minor earthquake. A split of tectonic plates. As we search for the blazing pillar of fire to fuel our creativity, we'll encounter more than one wilderness season threatening to hide the light.

After six weeks flat on my back from severe whooping cough, I returned to the entertainment company ready to get back to work. On the first day, I realized I wasn't where I was supposed to be. It was a minor earthquake, since the opportunity to grow in my career hung in the balance. I had the strange sense that wonder was somewhere else. I made another tough choice. It was time to dig deep for the courage to fully experience the call Presence had placed on my life.

Before leaving the company, I sat across from one of the partners. "I'm a storyteller," I said boldly, "so I'm going to dive in headfirst and see where it takes me. And I'm going to write novels." He was a dreamer too. But I'm not sure even I convinced him that my dream was real.

A whisper on the Zambezi, sparks of inspiration when flat on my back from sickness, stories planted in my soul from my world travels, and the people encountered among so many cultures. Each experience influenced the characters and settings I'd write one day. A choice was a revelation, digging into the dirt and planting a few more seeds. In the margins, it sounded like an insane decision. It wasn't strategic. It wasn't a calculated career move. It was a step into an unknown season that would challenge me beyond my expectations.

If you chase the light into the wild, it will test you.

My journey through wilderness seasons has been far from perfect. While I wasn't being chased across the desert by a vengeful pharaoh, I was wrestling with Presence. I made a bold declaration, and then the real world smacked me in the face. What was I thinking? Doubt. Uncertainty. Second-guessing. Wrapped in a package stuffed with responsibilities, expectations, and an underlying fear it was all going to crash and burn.

At the same time, an opportunity surfaced to executive produce a live record at one of the most prominent megachurches alongside a partner from my ministry years. Maybe there was unfinished business. Maybe I was reaching back once more toward past successes. Maybe the fear of stepping out on my own made the decision. Maybe I believed a little comfort was wise.

Why risk everything again?

The recording captured an incredible night with thousands of worship leaders. However, months later my partner and I found ourselves facing a familiar crossroads. Success of the project didn't silence the deeper call pulling me further into the wild. So once more, I stepped out on my own without a Plan B and started my own creative house.

It sounds so brave, but I was broken.

In the quietness of the margins, I was being tested beyond the light.

Plenty of dark days surrounded me in obscurity.

During this season, I faced the shocking deaths of my father-in-law and my mom only a month apart. I found myself lost in the wild. Thirty days later, the finality of leaving a partnership where it belonged left me wandering aimlessly for a while. I questioned how many others faced a similar season in the margins and wondered how they made it through.

We traveled to Bodfish, California, for Mom's memorial. My parents had served as missionaries for twenty years and had then served decades more in their denomination after returning to the States. I watched them sacrifice everything in ministry, so there was a heaviness surrounding the years leading up to Mom's death. She battled depression for a very long time and never fully returned to who she had once been, who I remembered.

As the room filled with people, most of whom I didn't recognize, I stared at rows of flowers near the front of the room. Churches and friends from all over the world showed their love in remembrance. Throughout the day, I noticed that most of the leaders who had served alongside my parents were absent. Not all. But most. Perhaps they found it easier to preach from a pulpit than to step with muddied boots onto the soil in the midst of the storm.

Presence and Creativity were guiding me toward a different path—one where the wilderness was an escape to revelation. A light flickered in the wild. A fire sparked my spirit. Presence was teaching me, forging me once again. My calling and creativity weren't for the applause, and the journey wasn't for the praises of man. That hadn't always been true for me, but determination to walk differently into the wilderness changed the course of my journey.

When we returned home, I carried Mom's memory and a renewed fire. A close friend invited me to camp out in his office to give me space to discover the path ahead. True friendship without expectation was a gift. Breakfasts at Tallyrand, a few blocks from NBC studios, were filled with laughter. No deadlines. No pressure. Just room to breathe. And in the stillness, my creativity stretched beyond the familiar. And there were others, lifelong friends who stood with me in the fire, surrounded me, prayed for me, and encouraged me.

This wilderness season wasn't easy, and it wasn't short. It was challenging, difficult, discouraging, enlightening, emboldening, and strengthening. In the margins, some days I wasn't sure what I was supposed to do next. Other days, frustration boiled beneath the surface when the path ahead seemed impossible. Months passed, pushing me to the brink of throwing in the towel. Perseverance wasn't a choice; it was a necessity. I refused to let go of the whisper in the wild nudging me to take just one more brave step.

Along with four friends, I boarded a plane to the Philippines to film a documentary entitled *The Invitation*. There were five of us on a creative mission. I returned to the soil, and hopefully, this time we wouldn't be riding around in an old VW Bug. On our first day of filming in the slums of Manila, we headed straight for Sitio Veterans—a city dump where families live in shanties stretched across numerous barrios. I'd been there before, so the welcome from the local pastors, children, and families was a much-needed bright light.

When I think about the margins—the overlooked and underestimated spaces where creativity is born—I picture Sitio Veterans. This was a place where the trajectory of my creativity refocused. What I'd chased for so long failed to bring fulfillment. Instead, I wrestled with where Presence was guiding me next. In this season of questioning, I walked the dirt roads of the slums as resilience was forged to chase the wonder of Presence above all else.

One of the most powerful stories we captured during those filming days was from a young woman who had grown up in Sitio Veterans. I'd first met Jessica years earlier when I was there with a different team, and she'd brought us to her home to meet her family in the barrio. She was a high school student at the time, working hard to achieve good grades. Her courage was evident as she showed us her certificates of achievement on the walls. But her family didn't have the resources to buy her schoolbooks. With tears in her eyes, she explained that instead of giving up, she had borrowed books from other students and transcribed every page into textbooks of her own.

Take a minute and wipe a tear.

I'll never forget the moment when she pulled stacks of handwritten notebooks off a shelf. Page after page, word after word, determination and resilience were scripted. It was light in the wild—a reminder that brilliance often begins where no one expects ... in obscurity.

Now, years later, I stood in her home again, this time with a camera crew capturing her story. By then, a scholarship fund had been established for children in Sitio Veterans. What began as one girl's persistence in the shadows became a flame spreading across her community. Those scholarships eventually grew into a school in the slums. Jessica and many others reached far beyond to inspire us all.

That's the truth of the margins.

Seeds planted in the dark grow into unexpected harvests. Light breaks out in wild places. And the stories born there—like Jessica's—remind us how creativity, resilience, determination, and calling rarely start in comfort. They start in the unseen, overlooked, impossible places everyone else has passed by in the wilderness.

The Israelites were familiar with the wild. It was the place of daily dependence. Manna at dawn, fire at night. For the prophets of old, the wilderness was the proving ground of their faith. For Jesus, it was the place of testing after He was baptized in the Jordan. Over and over again, Scripture reveals that the wild is never wasted. It's where Presence strips away what we thought we needed to survive and replaces it with Himself.

For the families of Sitio Veterans, the barrio was the wild: dirt roads that washed away in thunderstorms, shanties stacked and patched together, dreams dimmed by struggle. Yet in this place, light broke through. Parents carried a relentless faith as they fought for a brighter future. Children turned scarcity into determination, like transcribing textbooks by hand. Each one believed with a childlike faith that their future was not their present nor past. The light of Presence pierced the shadows, where seeds planted in hardship grew in hope.

Yes, the wild is uncomfortable. It's inconvenient. It's unpredictable. It's heartbreaking. But it's also exhilarating, groundbreaking, and soul-searching. A place where false lights burn out and true light shines. There are seasons when darkness presses in on all sides, but it's not the end of our story. In the wild, we whisper prayers as signals to courage unearthed through a deeper faith that outshines our fears. Here we find refuge, we find mission, and we find purpose.

Light is often clearest when everything else is dark. What others fear, we choose to embrace. We don't desire a platform; we embrace a calling. And the fire that Presence forges in us guides others to freedom. Creativity is born in the wild—unseen, uncelebrated, desperate, determined—but it's not a place of nothingness. It's a place where new dreams and visions are born in the light.

Not every journey into the wild is chosen; some are forced upon us. Hagar knew what it was to be cast into the wild. Sent into the desert with her son, Ishmael, she wandered with no plan or provision. The heat pressed down, the water ran out, and despair overwhelmed. She placed her boy under a bush, unable to watch him die. In that moment, Presence showed up. He opened her eyes to a well of water and spoke over her a future she never imagined. In the wild, she gave Presence a name: El Roi, "the God who sees me" (see Gen. 16:7–13 and 21:9–19).

Hagar's story is a reminder of how even in rejection and abandonment, the light of Presence shines upon us in the margins. The wild becomes a season of encounters where we are seen by Him, known by Him, and reminded that we are not alone. We believe it's a place where dreams go to die, when in reality it's where calling comes alive. Creativity isn't confined to familiar places. It flourishes in the margins—in the wild where comfort ends and faith begins.

The Israelites learned this under desert skies. Families in Sitio Veterans revealed this truth through their lives. Hagar named it in the depths of her despair. Along my journey in the wild, I've encountered it too—in an empty office where creativity was given room to breathe and in the slums of Manila where inspiration sparked brighter than ever before.

Candlelight shimmering into a pillar of fire.

Light in the wild is a reminder from Presence that our calling isn't forged in comfort. It's not defined by applause or anchored in past success—or even the opinions of this world. Our calling is shaped in obscurity, tested in stillness, forged in fire, and revealed in the light found in unexpected places.

> You're here to be light, bringing out the God-colors in the world. (Matt. 5:14a)

The world doesn't need more echo chambers—it's desperate for creatives with courage to disrupt. Our most powerful work may not be created in studios or sanctuaries; it may be born in the tension, the raw, the messy, and the magnificently real. That's where the wild lives. That's where the light is needed most.

We have a choice: wild or comfortable.

Will we carry the light or be left in the dark?

True creatives who choose the wild don't wait for validation. Their authentic creativity breaks through in boardrooms, classrooms, film sets, sound stages, recording studios, social platforms, and the streets of the forgotten. The art of the margins teaches us that creativity isn't about fitting in—it's about breaking through. Our work doesn't need permission; it just needs to be true. And when truth meets beauty in the world, culture shifts on their tectonic plates.

We were never meant to stay where it's comfortable.

Our light was made to shine in the wild.

5

EDGE OF BRAVE

"I'm an old woman, sick and tired of the voices rattling in my head. I am ready for this day, my final hours before I disappear into the hereafter ... my days have grown faded, blurry, run together in an endless sea of confusion. It's hard to distinguish what is real anymore. There are only a few things I still recognize as reality, things I will take to the grave."[2]

Before every breakthrough, there's the threshold. A blank page. A vacant studio. An empty office. A dwindling bank account. It's where one decision could change the trajectory of our creativity. But fear is waiting, whispering, daring us to turn back. It doesn't always appear as a monster. More often, it's subtle. A pause in a decision. A tightening in the chest. A hesitation in our hands before we pick up a pen, ready our brush, strum a chord, unmute the mic, or share our idea.

We believe fear is a threat to our creativity. It's the twinge on the back of our neck. It's the butterflies in our stomach. It's a warning to stop and go no further. But sometimes fear is the catalyst for change. Fear and doubt don't haunt work that's hollow—they haunt the work that holds weight. They haunt the creativity that's already growing beneath the soil.

Whenever I sit down to write or step into a new creative endeavor, there's a twinge in my spirit that questions whether my storytelling and creativity will resonate. I've stepped onto sets with crews gathered, wondering whether the doubt in my gut will ever leave. I've produced musicians and vocalists in the studio and stepped over the threshold into the unknown as fear and doubt faded in the mix. In those moments, the choice was to walk closer to the edge of brave.

Doubt leaves us questioning our calling. Fear threatens to stop us from discovering deeper creativity. Both show up not when we're coasting, but when we're risking something real. A thousand doubts close in from every direction, and some leave us paralyzed. But courage crosses the threshold to change everything. That should make us pay attention.

I started the creative house with nothing more than a desk, a laptop, and my cell phone. No clients. No projects. No safety net. Definitely no five-year plan. Doubt and fear were real, and the risks jutted upward like sheer cliffs. But there were stories I wanted to write, projects I wanted to produce, and creative avenues I wanted to explore. And I dreamed that those stories and endeavors would not only be entertaining but also carry the weight of something deeper.

Success was about more than survival. It was about digging creative ditches. It was about planting seeds in my calling. It was about watering patches of dirt in the wild.

When we create from the honesty of our soul, we expose a sacred calling. That vulnerability invites resistance, but it also invites revelation. The most meaningful art, the most dangerous ideas, the most daring expressions—they're never forged in our safe places. They're born in the fire, in the risks, in our trust that Presence stands with us in the flames. We don't have to be fearless. We don't have to surrender to doubt as it wraps itself around our creativity. We just have to keep digging, keep planting, keep watering those patches of dirt through the fear. And when the seeds grow, our hearts are illuminated by the presence of Creativity.

The words at the beginning of this chapter are the opening lines of my first novel. When I stared at a blank page and stood on the edge of brave, doubt swarmed like a ravaged beast. The spark came quietly, not like a host of angels singing. I wasn't sure I could trust the whisper. Deep pain and loss carried a story from my soul to my imagination. At first, it was flashes. Fragments. A single image. A sentence, then two. An old woman's voice echoed, and the words and world began to flow as if I were simply listening to a conversation.

But this first paragraph stopped me cold. I was haunted because I knew what would be required of me to write this story. Fear growled and sneered. Doubt rattled my instincts. This was the moment when breakthrough barged in, took a seat, and dared me to keep going.

The opening words unnerved me. Too raw. Too vulnerable. Too close to the edge.

In the margins, the story pulled from the roots of my past with a sharp resistance: *What if I fail? What if no one reads this? What if I'm not good enough?*

Night after night, week after week, month after month, doubt and fear hunted me. Pages turned into chapters and chapters into a rough draft. Not perfect, but the bones of the story were on the page. The louder the fear and doubt, the more determined I was to stand on the edge of brave. Fear was a sign. I was stepping closer to sacred ground—to my unique calling as a creative.

No one else knew about the old woman. No one. Commitment. Endurance. A relentless wonder to discover where her story would lead me. One sentence. One page. One late-night writing session at a time. I wrote anywhere and everywhere. Fear and doubt began as a compass, but as the story unfolded, I discovered how Presence in the art of the margins was my guide. The closer I was drawn to His path, the more creatively the story flowed out of me.

Writing my first novel birthed an entirely new creative season in my life. I wasn't chasing success; I was chasing wonder. Fear wasn't a sheer cliff. Doubt wasn't the final burial. When I stepped over the threshold, the edge of brave welcomed me to my calling. One step brought a breakthrough, even when I didn't know what might happen once the story was finished. Deep down, there was no other choice but obedience.

You might be thinking this is the part of the story where the novel lands on an editor's desk and rockets to the bestseller list. Wouldn't that be a perfect ending? But without an agent or any connections in the publishing world, my only path forward was to out-trust my fear. The odds were against me, so all I could do was surrender the story and the outcome.

As an indie, typos and all, the margins took me deeper. The story gained traction and a following grew as I embarked on a book tour with Barnes & Noble.

I'll never forget the first store. I was scared to death to talk to anyone. No one believes I'm an introvert ... except for me. But this story was birthed in a whisper, so there was no other choice but to fight the fear and slay the doubt. It wasn't until halfway through the book tour that I began to find my voice to connect with people. And when the tour was over, I stepped through the doorway to another story with more bravery.

Success wasn't about book sales or notoriety. It was rooted in the art of the margins—courage, obedience, and surrender. My calling was to be a storyteller, dreamer, believer, fear fighter, and doubt killer. If I'd surrendered to fear and doubt, then I'd still be staring at a blank page.

And I'm not alone. Scripture is filled with moments when fear and doubt became a doorway to the edge of brave. Esther stood before the king with her people's lives on the line. She knew one wrong step could cost everything. Fear was deadly. Yet courage pushed her forward into the light of her heritage. That single act of bravery birthed a breakthrough for an entire nation. (See the book of Esther.)

In Judges 4, we see Jael, an ordinary woman hiding in her tent, confronted with extraordinary circumstances. She didn't have rank, training, or status. But she had courage. And in her decisive act, history turned when she killed Sisera, the Canaanites' commander.

Paul reminds us in 2 Timothy, "For God did not give us a spirit of fear. He gave us a spirit of power and of love and of a good mind" (1:7 NLV). Fear doesn't define our calling. Doubt doesn't imprison our creativity. In the wild, courage and clarity in Presence unleash what's buried beneath the soil.

Over and over, Scripture reminds us that courage is not the absence of fear: It's the movement through fear. It's the Israelites fleeing for their lives with a pillar of fire by night. No matter how strong their belief might've been previously, doubt swarmed through the whole tribe when they reached the impassable Red Sea. Then the water rose and parted, leaving the seabed dry.

And once they had walked safely to the other side, the sea wiped out the root of their fear.

Courage is faith with trembling hands and obedience to choose the edge of brave when we step across the threshold as our knees shake.

Years ago, we were on vacation in Hawaii, staying on the North Shore a few miles from an airfield. On the first day at 6 a.m., the wife woke up with a strange request. She wanted to go skydiving. Let me say that one more time: skydiving. To fully appreciate how shocking the request was, you need to know for the entire flight over the Pacific, she had kept a vise grip on my hand every time there was the slightest turbulence.

Now, I had a choice to make: talk her out of it or drive her to the airfield.

I did what any seasoned husband would do. I got the keys and started the car.

We arrived at the airfield and inquired about what we needed to do to make this dream happen. A woman behind the counter explained there was a short training for tandem dives (with the swipe of a card), and basically, that was it. When she slid a stack of papers across the counter, we were at the point of no return.

Door one: fear. Door two: doubt. Door three: courage.

Which one was the wife going to choose?

As she read through the papers before signing, I stopped her and explained what the documents contained. "Basically, if the parachute doesn't open, it's not their fault."

Even my pointed words didn't deter her from choosing door number three. While she headed inside a hangar for "training," I sat on a bench and held her purse. I chuckled because I was certain I looked like so many husbands at the mall who did the same. Curious, I stepped over to the doorway of the hangar and listened as several skydivers walked through a twenty-minute training as the wife stood ready with a harness secured around her waist.

This was really happening. No refunds.

My heart pounded as she walked across the airfield to a waiting plane. Within minutes, the plane was airborne before disappearing into the clouds. For what seemed like an eternity, I kept my sights fixed toward the sky, wondering whether she was really going to jump.

Was she going to cross the threshold and meet her fear head on?

Ten minutes later, several parachutes appeared, soaring across clear blue skies. I heard the wife's voice shouting, and laughter followed. Back and forth the parachute swung until the tandem approached the ground at a rapid pace. It wasn't a ballerina landing. Both hit the grass and tumbled, and I was certain she was hurt. As I stepped toward the grass, she bounced up and shouted toward me, "I want to go again!"

Yes, she jumped not once but twice.

She remains one of the bravest people I know.

Sometimes the leap itself rewrites the story we believe is true about our limits. Fear says, "Don't try." Courage whispers, "Jump anyway." Courage doesn't always look like slaying giants. In moments like these, it looks like saying yes to one impossible step.

Every journey worth taking in the margins begins with hesitation. A pause where fear pulls us back toward safety, toward the familiar, and offers us a thousand reasons to settle. *It's too risky. You're not ready. Others have already done better. What if the parachute doesn't open?*

Standing at the edge of brave, many stories end before they've even begun. Ideas are buried. Songs go unsung. Stories remain untold. Breakthrough for an entire nation would never have occurred. A decisive act would never have altered history. Creativity would have never become a weapon against fear. Stepping out of a plane into the beauty of creation would never have brought freedom to soar among the clouds.

Fear wins if we choose to never step toward the edge of brave. The truth is, our story never really lives until we say yes in the face of fear. In that moment of surrender—stepping into the unknown with courage—that's what sets our creativity in motion.

If you've ever felt paralyzed by fear at the starting point—good. It's not a sign you're unqualified. It's not a sign failure is right around the corner. It's not a sign to turn back. It's a sign your creativity is alive and it's time to jump.

Fear attacks not because you're empty but because the creativity within is rooted beneath the soil of holy ground. *Your creativity can reshape the world.* Repeat: Your creativity can reshape the world. Imagine the adventure that awaits at the edge of brave. In the margins, the battleground isn't the page or the stage; it's in your mind and heart.

Fear asks, "What if you fail?" Courage answers, "What if this changes everything?" When fear says, "You're not ready," faith answers, "Maybe not—but I'm willing." Fear demands perfection and a certain outcome before you begin. Creativity dares you to begin anyway.

The most meaningful art, the most daring ideas, and the most dangerous expressions are not born in comfort. They're born when you're afraid to fly, then jump out of a plane. They're born in the fires of bravery and courage. Imagine a forge: heat, pressure, hammering, sparks flying. That's where weapons and tools are shaped. The same is true of creativity in the margins. Fear is also part of the fire. And the flames make us stronger because we are not standing alone.

In the wild, we don't have to be fearless. We only need to cross the threshold. To write the next line. To stand strong when our voice shakes. To risk sharing what matters most through our creativity. Imagine painting breakthrough after breakthrough on your canvas, especially those where fear and doubt stood in the way. Each brushstroke is terrifying. Each color feels too bold. But fear and doubt were not the signal to stop—they were the compass to press forward in the wild toward the edge of brave.

When fear and doubt hunt us in the wilderness, and both will, we can return to Paul's words: "For God did not give us a spirit of fear. He gave us a spirit of power and of love and of a good mind" (2 Tim. 1:7 NLV). We may stand at the edge. But so does power. So does love. So does clarity of mind. And so does Presence.

In the margins, which whisper will we follow?

As creatives, we can be the fear fighters and doubt killers. We don't need to wait until those disappear. We need to simply take each courageous step with trembling hands, a steady gaze, and a surrendered heart. In our creativity, we can find refuge on sacred and holy ground because there is no turning back from the edge of brave. We can walk through the wilderness to the other side with courage. We can jump when we don't know how far we will free-fall ... and pull the rip cord before we crash land.

6

THE WILDERNESS SEASON

On the early morning phone call, Dad's voice cracked with panic—he couldn't find Mom. Within minutes, I was behind the wheel headed toward their house. He called again saying that a hospital in Hollywood had reached him with the shocking news that she'd been admitted to the emergency room. We later found out she had left the apartment before sunrise, crossed the street, and jumped off a bridge into Echo Park Lake.

While it wasn't a tall bridge, she had never learned to swim. Two men who were fishing in the early hours pulled her out of the water. Neither left a name when the paramedics arrived. To this day, we don't know who they were. All we know is without them, she would've drowned.

By the time we reached the hospital, the fog had closed in. Shock. Disbelief. Silence. And definitely tension among everyone who was present. Before we even had a chance to wrap our minds around what was happening, Mom was transferred to a psychiatric facility in Glendale. For the next forty days, she was on mandatory lockdown. Her gaze fixed on the white walls. Her voice muted. Totally unresponsive. Word spread to friends, family, and leaders through our denomination, and the responses varied.

One afternoon, I went to visit her alone. For an hour, she said nothing. Just stared. As I rose to leave, she climbed out of bed and followed me. I glanced over my shoulder and stopped in the hallway. She was only a few steps behind. Knowing she wasn't allowed to leave, a nurse approached to usher her back to her room. When the exit doors opened, I glanced back once more as a frail voice broke through the silence.

"Don't leave me here."

Those words still ring in my ears. Her plea broke me as the doors closed and locked. As I left her on the other side, anger and hatred filled my veins. I loved my mom, but I hated where she had ended up. I needed someone to blame. And I wanted someone to explain how this happened. I wanted Presence to give me some answers. I wanted Mom to walk out of lockdown totally healed.

Thousands of years earlier, a dry and merciless desert stretched endlessly in the wilderness. Worn from battle, Elijah sought shade beneath a broom bush, convinced that his story was over. "Enough of this, God! Take my life—I'm ready to join my ancestors in the grave!" (1 Kings 19:4b).

Elijah wandered in the wilderness.

"Enough of this, God!"

A cave—shelter. A cry—surrender.

Forty days. Forty nights.

Hurricane winds whipped. Boulders shattered. An earthquake rumbled. A fire erupted. In the wilderness, Presence whispered louder than them all. Perhaps our greatest fear is being left alone in the wilderness. But the margins, the wild of our creativity, in seasons of obscurity, isn't where the story ends. Even in brokenness, it's where a new story begins.

Mom spent forty days and nights in lockdown, and many wilderness seasons followed. I believe she was worn from battle and the weight of ministry. She was desperate to escape. She was convinced her story had ended and made a choice she regretted. One she was judged for the rest of her days until her final breath brought her to the other side. In her pain, she surrendered the only way she knew how, because admitting her struggles within the circles of leadership would've been equally shattering.

My parents' world shrank when she was released from the psychiatric ward the first time, and with each return that followed. Of course, everyone prayed for healing, but the number of those who stayed close grew smaller. A fracture between me and Dad that had existed for years only widened. Relational hurricanes whipped, family boulders shattered, disagreements rumbled like earthquakes, and a searing fire erupted between us.

Leaders who had served alongside my parents for decades chose distance instead of nearness. Fewer were willing to walk in the aftermath during the seasons when they were needed most. Dad's executive assistant was one who stayed by their side, no matter what was asked. I am forever grateful for her willingness to be present, for her sacrifice, and for her love for Mom.

And she wasn't the only one.

An unexpected visitor arrived after Mom was released the first time. A friend of my parents. An A-list celebrity. A fellow creative. Now, I don't share this lightly. No name is needed. She was one of the few who showed up when others drifted away.

At the time, her latest film was being shredded by church leaders. Yet she came anyway. She sat in my parents' living room. She stayed with Mom. While others judged her for her creative decisions, convicting her as morally bankrupt, she walked alongside us in the wilderness without fanfare, a pulpit, or an entourage. Her presence resonated louder than any sermon.

> All praise to the God and Father of our Master, Jesus the Messiah! Father of all mercy! God of all healing counsel! He comes alongside us when we go through hard times, and before you know it, he brings us alongside someone else who is going through hard times so that we can be there for that person just as God was there for us. (2 Cor. 1:3–4)

An assistant. An A-lister. The few who were brave enough.

Mom battled depression for many years. She was in and out of psychiatric facilities numerous times. Holidays were especially tough whenever we visited her in those places. She fought silence and pain with moments of courage and a flare in her gaze. I'm convinced healing was waiting on the other side. But I've also questioned whether the sacrifice in ministry was worth the aftermath. While that may leave the religious shifting uncomfortably in their seats, it's the truth of the struggle. Far too many who have sacrificed in the church are left behind in the wilderness—alone.

In this season, I encountered an unexpected creativity pouring out through story as an altar of surrender. When the last page was written, I dedicated *The Disillusioned* to Mom. Not only to honor her as a son, but to honor her courage until the end. Regardless of her struggles, she chose to be brave. She never stopped fighting, even when others gazed upon her with pity. She remains one of the cornerstones of why I'm a storyteller and creative today.

What I've learned from an assistant, an A-lister, and the apostle Paul is that creatives in the wilderness seasons need fellow wanderers. We can't wait until all hell breaks loose before we travel alongside another to pick up the shattered pieces. And we can't call ourselves leaders if we are not willing to walk with those who are journeying through the darkness.

The aftermath of Mom's passing and the wilderness season that followed nearly broke me. Financially. Emotionally. Spiritually. One leader offered some advice: You can always sell your house and move to the Philippines. Those words only fueled my determination to dig deeper. I wasn't going to back down. I wasn't going to listen to anyone who wasn't walking in the wilderness with others. And I wasn't going to become a religious statue in the wild either.

Instead, I buried a few more seeds beneath the soil.

In my years in ministry, I've noticed how oftentimes influential leaders avoid engaging unless you're someone important. I'd experienced this firsthand many times, and I'd seen the same with Mom. That perspective shifted my journey as a creative and how I've chosen to walk with those around me. Not every encounter needs to be posted on social.

As leaders in the wild, status and titles mean nothing unless there is substance in serving in the margins. Leaders who choose to lead must be willing to walk in the wild with others throughout the seasons, not when it's convenient but when it's disruptive. That means beyond the pulpit, beyond the spotlight, beyond the boardroom. That's where the real story begins, that's where obscurity wages war, that's where the only creative reward is to serve.

As creatives, our hope is not built on acceptance or the praises of man. Our creativity is not rooted in a uniquely gifted leader. In the wilderness, our creative journey inspires us toward a deeper calling. And when we walk alongside fellow wanderers in the midst of those seasons, there is a community who will stand with us in the fire. We'll dig creative ditches—day after day, one shovel at a time. We'll go unnoticed by the world, but not by those who are walking with us.

Together, we shout, "Enough of this, God!"

Presence promises to meet us in the wild. He hears our prayers. He provides in unexplainable ways. In the driest of seasons, He uses our lives to create and walk alongside others no matter their circumstances or struggles. Presence refines our lives in the flames and deepens our calling when we chase more than a mirage. We'll fight for every word. We'll stand in wonder at the colors of our canvas. We'll kneel in the dirt and lay our lives at His feet. There is no better place to be than in His presence with fellow wanderers.

Some days will be brutal. Others will be exhilarating. But the wilderness is where breakthrough and freedom await. Voices are refined. Courage is forged. Destiny is shaped.

When we see no way to be free, when we call out to Presence in our brokenness, He redeems us. It may not look like what the world wants, or what the church expects, but it is truth. He resurrects and restores our faith. Our creativity expresses itself in more meaningful ways. In the hidden places, in obscurity, He prepares us with an unrelenting determination and resilience to go beyond the edge of brave.

Everything false is stripped away. Success. Security. Surety. Spirituality.

Everything true remains. Scars. Sacrifice. Sojourn. Sanctity.

In the wilderness, the art of the margins reveals creativity born not in what's false, but in what's true. We may feel abandoned, but we're already found. We may not know the way, but we're walking in the footsteps of the Waymaker. We may struggle, we may fall, but we're not on this journey alone as we wander deeper into the wild. The wilderness strips away the noise, the distractions, the doubts, the anger, so when the spark of creativity strikes, it's deeper, fuller, and rooted in who we've become in the infernos of life.

Whether it's forty days or forty years, an epic journey of creativity chases courage, determination, inspiration, a deeper and truer faith—not rooted in religion, but in a relationship with Presence. Creativity revealed isn't about what we create; it's rooted in who created us. His voice resonates clearly in our calling, our purpose sharpens, and we walk in the wild stronger with fellow wanderers.

Forged out of these wilderness wanderings are resilience and bravery. Whatever caves we find ourselves chained in along the journey will prepare our souls to express raw, unfiltered, authentic creativity. Because these wilderness seasons aren't punishment: They're preparation.

When our momentum slows, our vision blurs, our path disappears, we can feel like our creative souls are suffering. We wander aimlessly. We hide away. We struggle to find inspiration. We surrender to our fears. But if we step across the threshold, if we embrace the edge of brave with wonder, then our creative souls are forged in holy fire.

In the stillness of our uncertainty, agony, reverie, or failure, we listen for a whisper, and maybe even a resounding shout, as we stretch beyond ourselves. Failure and obscurity in the wild forge greater faith in Presence and leave us more aware of wanderers traveling around us. In the wilderness—where most give up—something deeper forms in the fire.

Resolve. Empathy. Wisdom. Vision.

Our failures make us humble. Our grief makes us tender. Our obscurity makes us clear-eyed. In the margins, the storms of the wilderness do not define us; they simply reveal that we have been forged in silence, sorrow, and struggle. And in those seasons, we discover the wild is the birthplace of destiny.

Every season ends with a turning.

Elijah returned from the desert to confront a king.

Mom's life and death fueled my courage as a storyteller.

The wilderness is never wasted—it's always forging, even when unseen. Grief becomes voice. Pain becomes depth. Obscurity becomes preparation. When Presence calls our name, we step forward not because we are fearless or unbroken but because we are unshaken. The wilderness doesn't take us out—it takes us deeper. It strips away illusions. It dismantles false strength. It separates lies from truth. It sifts relationships. And it leaves us rooted in Presence, the One who called us and forges resilience in our souls.

The wilderness is not the end of the story: It's the threshold toward the edge of brave. Step deeper humbly, tenderly, clear-eyed. Wander in the margins because what looks like desolation may be the ground of your greatest becoming.

So, embrace the wilderness seasons. Don't rush past the silence. Welcome the hardship and know you will be stronger for it. Let the ache shape your voice. Allow the wild to dig wells of empathy, vision, and endurance in your soul. Because what feels like loss is often the birthplace of new life. And what feels like the wasteland may be the canvas where Presence paints your next masterpiece.

7

A BLANK PAGE IS STILL A BEGINNING

The cursor blinked against a white screen. Steady. Relentless. Almost cruel. I was tucked in a window seat on a flight across the country, and the longer the cursor flashed, the louder it seemed to shout back at me: Do you really have something worth saying?

The screaming of babies only intensified in the cabin.

A bit of turbulence rattled the aircraft as I shifted in my seat. A Hans Zimmer soundtrack blasted in my ears, only amplifying the tension. A half dozen documents were open on my laptop—ideas, fragments, dialogue, descriptions of realms locked in my imagination. None of it felt like enough. None of it was worth keeping. Yet the idea, the vision, the inspiration, the voice refused to let go. And there was an intense pressure, an impossible challenge, an unrelenting sense of torture.

As creatives, we know this moment. Agony and torture are found in the silence of a blank page. A hush before something begins. A stillness that seems to last forever. Anticipation where possibility and fear collide. A glimpse of a breakthrough. Vast and limitless. Also intimidating and suffocating. Uncluttered yet heavy with questions and possibilities.

Just breathe. Inhale Presence. Exhale Creativity.

A blank page doesn't ask what you'll create—it asks who you are. Fearless, brave, determined, courageous, surrendered? It demands honesty in raw truth. It exposes insecurities you thought were buried. And it whispers questions that land like bombs dropping from thirty thousand feet. Are you ready? Will this matter? What if you fail again? Is this impossible?

Whether literal or metaphorical, the blank page is the most honest mirror of a creative's soul. It shows us not only what we hope to create but also what we fear will never come alive.

On the flight to Los Angeles, another hour passed as a young couple across the aisle in the row ahead struggled to calm their triplet babies. Yes, triplets! The screaming elevated. Wild human instruments interrupted Zimmer's encompassing score and my attempt to conquer the page. I stopped for a moment and watched as an elderly woman seated in the same row as the couple leaned over and offered to hold one of the babies.

Surrendering, the mom handed over one of her children, and the screaming lessened. The flight continued late into the night as peace spread throughout the cabin. Relief. Then the words began to flow, and a new world emerged.

A blank page rarely comes with clarity, and yet the story swirling in my imagination remained vivid. This one didn't announce itself with trumpets, road maps, or angels singing "Hallelujah." Only the voices echoed. The blank page arrived clothed in tension, and the words followed, rooted in expectation. A wicked combination, in the best of ways, to push me beyond staring with eternal uncertainty. In a new beginning, the impossible became possible.

Maybe you've faced a similar moment, minus the screaming triplets, when what stared back at you dissolved into clarity. A new job that didn't feel like yours ... until you experienced your first win. A move that unsettled more than excited, until you found community. A diagnosis that forced you to hit pause, until remission readied you to conquer the world. A call to faith that didn't give you the full plan, until you experienced the next step through the gentle whisper of Presence.

That tension is sacred.

In the margins, tension means we're stepping into a future not yet seen. We're risking our creativity, our craft, our calling to discover something eternal. It means we're alive enough to stand on the edge of brave and take one more step, even if we're scared out of our mind.

The irony is we often despise the tension of blank pages. We avoid them. We fill them with distractions, or we wait for inspiration to arrive fully formed. We fear them, yet we crave what they hold. We wait for them to speak while refusing to write a single word. We despise their silence yet demand they sing. We long for brilliance but dread the cost. The beauty of the blank page isn't in what's written—it's in what could be, who we could become in the process.

A young couple boards a flight with screaming triplets: a blank page. A stranger offers a helping hand: the beauty of what could be. Each one willing to change because of the tension.

In those moments of uncertainty, the blank page is less a void than an altar. It's a place where fear is surrendered, where what's false begins to fade away. It's where creativity is forged in the flames of courage. One step. One word. One act. One helping hand. We don't need the whole manifesto. We don't need an entire outline (shout-out to the improvisers out there). We don't need to know the happily ever after. We just need the courage to take the next brave step.

For me, the blank page begins with a spark. Not a manuscript. Not even a chapter. Just an idea—fragile and unfinished. One idea turns into words when I least expect it, like a whisper refusing to leave on a late-night flight. An image of a boy caught between worlds, standing on the edge of a vast and dangerous secret. That was the spark. No character beyond a shadow. Just a flicker. A question. A haunting possibility. Then the boy spoke, and the page was blank no more.

Fragments scribbled in notebooks, ideas typed into my laptop and iPad. Jotted scenes. Shredded, dead-end beginnings tossed in the trash. Each attempt to build on the story—to write the first chapter—left the pieces collapsed. Pages piled up, but none of them were right. What I carried in my mind never survived the journey from my imagination to the page.

Until the screaming stopped.

What do many of us do when faced with a blank page? We push it aside. We're convinced it's not the right time to begin. We tell ourselves we're not the right person to pull off such a monumental task. In the noise of life, we bury our creativity deep beneath the soil, yet it remains a seed.

For years, this story never left me. The spark kept igniting, even though the blank page remained intimidating. In the middle of creative meetings, production shoots, cross-country flights, workouts, LA traffic, and sleepless nights, the blank page asked: What if?

The idea drifted in limbo after countless false starts. I'd get one or two chapters into the story, then the wilderness buried the seed again. Waiting. Brewing. Haunting. The truth is, part of me was afraid to commit, because beginnings expose our creativity. A new project feels fragile, and for many creatives, that is frightening. It's easier to say, "I'll start tomorrow," than risk failing now. Oftentimes our wilderness seasons last longer than we hoped—much like the Israelites. We become comfortable and settle for standing still in the sands of the wild.

Beneath the soil, the supernatural boy never stopped clawing to the surface.

Presence has a way of using silence and the wilderness to grow us. What feels like delay is actually formation. What feels like failure is preparation. What feels like a blank page is Presence clearing space for the seed to blossom. What feels like screaming triplets is actually a breakthrough to another world.

While the draft pages stacked up, my skill as a writer wasn't yet strong enough to pull off the story in my imagination. But my craft sharpened with each word, and my voice as a storyteller began to resonate in my soul. Slowly, almost imperceptibly, the seed of an original idea grew beneath the soil. Characters welcomed names. A world began to take shape, and other realms formed. I learned to listen intently, and the boy between two worlds shared his voice with me—an invitation from Presence and a gift of creativity.

Nearly a decade later, this spark would become a trilogy—those blank pages turned into bound books on the shelves and in the cloud. But the journey began with surrendering to the first page, even when the screaming was too loud. For me, the supernatural fantasy series became more than a story about a boy named Jack. It turned into an adventure in the wild beyond my expectations where I explored creative limits, inviting threads of hope and love onto the page. I never imagined how hard I would fight to keep the story alive, but the blank pages weren't a curse—they were a promise of calling.

No matter the struggle, the heartache, the obstacles, the impossibles—blank pages force us to trust that Presence will turn whispers into words, sparks into epics, and beginnings into greatness.

Years ago, I was seated inside the David Geffen Theater on the Academy lot watching a private screening of *Blade Runner 2049*. One of the greatest theater experiences of my life. At the end of the film, there was an interview onstage with the director, screenwriter, special effects supervisor, and composer. I leaned forward when Hans Zimmer spoke. My mind flashed to the late-night flight home and the blank page of what would become the *Beacon Hill* trilogy. After the interview, I had an opportunity to meet one of the greatest composers of all time. I'm sure he'll never remember me, but it was a moment where Presence showed me the blank page is still the beginning of greatness.

The margins are where faith, art, and courage collide.

Abraham knew this well. Scripture says, "By an act of faith, Abraham said yes to God's call to travel to an unknown place that would become his home. When he left he had no idea where he was going" (Heb. 11:8).

His story didn't begin with the end in mind; it began with a blank horizon. He left home with no GPS, no timeline, no master plan—just a whisper from Presence and a willingness to trust. This was the first step of his blank page.

Centuries later, in an attic in Amsterdam, a teenager stared down her own blank page. Anne Frank filled her notebook with words no one expected to survive. Her pages weren't polished drafts; they were the raw honesty of adolescence colliding with fear, hiding with hope. She never knew her diary would outlive her. The legacy of her blank page offers proof that what feels fragile today can echo for generations.

Once upon a time rarely reveals the *happily ever after*.

What we create today will live beyond us.

Long before hobbits and elves made their way into our imaginations, J. R. R. Tolkien was a soldier in World War I. He carried mud and blood in his memories, watched friends die in the trenches, and trudged through fields littered with the cost of humanity's worst instincts.

Tolkien turned to the blank page and penned mythologies that gave language to courage, loss, friendship, and the fight against the darkest evils. His creativity wasn't entertainment or escapism—it was survival rooted in encounters. His blank page became maps of Middle-earth.

Like millions of other *Lord of the Rings* fans, I own the collection of books and the extended versions of the films, including hours of behind-the-scenes footage featuring Peter Jackson and the geniuses at Wētā Workshop. Learning about the impossible feat they pulled off is nearly as entertaining as the films themselves. To this day, Tolkien's trilogy remains a timeless, epic tale.

What binds these creatives is not genius or circumstance; it's faith. Faith to step onto the blank page when the outcome is unknown. Faith to believe what starts small may someday matter. Faith that the unseen work is not wasted in the margins ... because a blank page is where legacies are born, where greatness is unearthed. Whether in the deserts of an ancient world, the silence of an attic, or the battlefields of Europe, our creativity belongs in the wild alongside those creatives who have gone before us.

Every story needs a voice of wisdom—someone to hand us the tools we don't yet know how to use. Oftentimes, when we need a guide the most, no one shows up. That's how beginnings feel. The blank page waits, but no one steps alongside to walk with us. No hand reaches out with a map. No voice offers reassurance. Just silence. Just fear. Just a page daring us to run free. But in the margins, we're never alone.

> Look at me. I stand at the door. I knock. If you hear me call and open the door, I'll come right in and sit down to supper with you. Conquerors will sit alongside me at the head table, just as I, having conquered, took the place of honor at the side of my Father. That's my gift to the conquerors! (Rev. 3:20–21)

In the absence of a worldly mentor, Presence reveals Himself as our guide. His whisper cuts through the silence: "Begin anyway." His Spirit meets us not with a map of the world but with courage. Not with religious formulas but with faith rooted in a relationship with Him.

Abraham said "Yes" in an act of faith, unsure of where he was going. Anne Frank listened to the whisper as she wrote in the attic, not knowing her words would be read by future generations. Tolkien heard the whisper in the trenches of battle, and he brought Middle-earth to life. Each one discovered how blank pages are new beginnings that forge resilience in the midst of uncertainty—the very wilderness where courage is born.

When the spark of a story haunted me, I waited for someone to affirm that I was ready to take the next step. No one came. Instead, Presence met me in the margins, and we wandered together. His unseen hand steadied me through the blank pages, failed drafts, and long nights of doubting I'd ever find my way. He walked with me when adversity threatened to derail my dream to write this epic story. I didn't always see Him in my mind, but I sensed Him in my soul.

In the margins, blank pages are never empty when they are surrendered at the altar of Presence. A place in the wild where we are refined, where insecurities are stripped away, and where we discover trust in His voice beyond our own doubt and creativity. It's where we learn to listen for Presence as He walks with us.

Still, the blank page will never stop feeling intimidating. Whether it's a manuscript, a film, a career shift, or a step of faith, new beginnings always feel like they might shatter into a million pieces. Blank pages expose us, whispering lies about our creative worth. But they are also an invitation toward deeper faith and more courageous creativity. The art of the margins teaches us there is always a choice.

Abraham wrote in sacrifice. Anne Frank wrote in uncertainty. Tolkien wrote in the light of destiny. My own quiet spark wrote beneath the soil through years of adversity before finally breaking through. When we've encountered the creative greatness of fellow wanderers in the wild, we are inspired to face the blank page with a deeper resolve and unrelenting courage.

Every one of our stories begins with a blank page. And every story is a reminder we don't need the whole map of the wild. We don't need all the answers. We don't need to know the *happily ever after*. All we need is the courage to take the next brave step toward *once upon a time*.

The blank page is staring back at you, but don't be fooled into believing it's empty. In the wilderness, it's holy ground. An altar. A canvas waiting to carry your obedience, your risk, your faith. Because a blank page is not the end of the story—it's an invitation to a new beginning.

Trust it. Trust Presence.

8

CREATE IT ANYWAY

A thunderous storm and raging seas surrendered to a radiant morning. Lucy stared at her reflection in a mirror after whispering a spell to make herself beautiful. In *The Chronicles of Narnia: The Voyage of the Dawn Treader*, she confronts her inner doubts as she sees a reflection of Susan, her older sister, instead of herself. A reflection of her jealousy and insecurity. It's a powerful moment when Aslan appears with a priceless reminder.

"You doubt your value. Don't run from who you are."[3]

Creativity is a mirror into our lives—it's our testimony.

We're taught to polish the work. Smooth the edges. Rewrite until it's perfect. Wait until it's finished and flawless before we show anyone. If we're going to impress, release only what won't embarrass us. Show the masterpiece, never the cracks. Post the highlight reels, never the blurred moments. Wear the trendiest fashion to fit in with culture. Scroll on the newest device. Say the right words or sing the right songs to be part of the conversation. Put on an outward facade to make the best impression.

But who do you see when you look in the mirror?

If I'm honest, there are days when a bald Nicolas Cage stares back.

On those days when buried doesn't mean dead, the margins call us to create it anyway. Presence guides us toward vulnerable expression through our creativity—more than words, more than trends, more than a canvas. Vulnerability is our testimony to create from places we've survived. For the unseen artist or the leader showing up in silence, vulnerable creative expression becomes an outpouring of our calling, more powerful than standing on a street corner holding a sign that reads, "Heaven or Hell?"

Creatives who truly carry weight—whose lives are making a lasting impact—are the ones who vulnerably pierce the noise, break down the walls, and ignite change. Rarely do they come with polish; they come from the trenches. From the workshop covered in dust from a new idea. From the late nights in an editing room where doubt lingers. From the scars we've tried to hide within the pages. From the keynote spilling truth that goes against the trends of culture. And from the wild, the margins, where we choose to create it anyway in an act of raw obedience.

Our scars have a voice in every broken chapter, every failed attempt, every piece of our journey that almost didn't make it. Each one carries a vulnerability others will relate to. Each one carries a truth others are desperate to experience. Someone else's breakthrough is waiting on our obedience in the margins. When we create it anyway, we encounter a forging of strength in our creative journey. It's in every brushstroke connecting our creation to another's soul.

In many ways, sharing only the highlight reel of the polished design, the seamless performance, the glossy pitch deck, or the smooth book cover isn't the courageous part of our testimony. What if we showed the messy draft, the raw lyric, the product design that still carried fingerprints of trial and error? What if we shared not only what we've created but what we've survived in the wild? Now, this doesn't mean starring in our own reality show and vomiting our deepest, darkest confessions to the world in hopes of gaining notoriety and fame. Vulnerability isn't about lifting ourselves up; rather, it's about encouraging others to press on in the fight.

In the margins, there's a holy exchange when we create in vulnerability as we pursue excellence in our craft. Shame loses its grip. Isolation breaks free. Temptation for attention is buried beneath the soil. And the cracks in our creativity become the very light where Presence shines through.

We don't have to wait until we've "made it" to share what we're creating. We don't have to have the whole canvas painted. Our testimony doesn't have to be perfect. In the margins, we can share our story, even with its rough edges. What matters most is that our creativity bleeds with honesty—our testimony planted vulnerably in the soil of authenticity.

When we choose to create it anyway, we allow our creativity to flow like a roaring river. We give ourselves the freedom to wander through the wild to explore, experience, and encounter the calling on our lives without staring at the wrong reflection.

In the margins, vulnerability is at the core of every creative act.

When an artist unveils a canvas, the brushstrokes carry not only color but confession. When an entrepreneur pitches an idea, they expose their dreams as possibilities that don't exist yet. When a writer pours words onto a page, it's an outpouring of their scars into a story. When a leader stands in front of a team and says, "I don't have all the answers, but we can figure it out if we work together," that's imperfection racing toward breakthrough.

In the margins, vulnerability leads to confession beyond culture. Confession reveals imperfection. Imperfection writes testimonies. Testimonies lead to breakthrough in our creativity, not only for us but for others as well.

As creatives, our hope is when we stare into the mirror, it's not simply our reflection we see but the reflection of Presence in us the world sees.

The first brushstroke, the first prototype, the first risk—it all feels like stepping onto a stage before the curtain rises. Our temptation is always the same: Hide the mess. Don't show the half-formed, the half-believed, the half-healed, the half-restored. If we are going to connect and resonate deeply through our creativity, we cannot begin from polished and perfect. We need to show the cracks, the risks that almost broke us.

Vulnerability opens up the unknown to unearth stories we never imagined, melodies and lyrics expressed with raw authenticity, and bold ideas the world believed were impossible. When we create it anyway, we're not guaranteed perfection, we're not guaranteed notoriety, and we're not guaranteed a reality show. But we are promised fulfillment.

In culture, scars resonate stronger than perfection. Others lean in when we allow them to see behind the curtain. When we step away from the pulpit and sit with them around a bonfire. When we share our journey in the wild searching for the edge of brave. The truth is our scars are not distractions from creativity—they're our testimony engrained in our creations. Moments when we struggled to grasp enough courage to take another step are the places where wanderers find strength to keep going along their own wilderness journey.

Paul wrote letters from prison cells. His body chained, his future on earth in the balance. Yet his words traveled through the centuries—vulnerable, confessional, imperfect, testimonial. Inked onto parchment in weakness, doubt, strength, and certainty. What he might have hidden, he gave anyway. Two thousand years later, his letters still encourage, challenge, inspire, and transform culture. His blank page was his testimony of creativity, so he created it anyway.

> Through your faithful prayers and the generous response of the Spirit of Jesus Christ, everything he wants to do in and through me will be done. I can hardly wait to continue on my course. I don't expect to be embarrassed in the least. On the contrary, everything happening to me in this jail only serves to make Christ more accurately known, regardless of whether I live or die. They didn't shut me up; they gave me a platform! Alive, I'm Christ's messenger; dead, I'm his prize. Life versus even more life! I can't lose. (Phil. 1:19–21)

In Acts 9:36–38, a woman named Tabitha (meaning "gazelle") quietly wove kindness into clothing for widows and cared for the overlooked. She was a disciple who served without an audience. When she died, some of the disciples went to Lydda to ask Peter to come with them. So he was taken to Tabitha's dead body.

> Her old friends, most of them widows, were in the room mourning. They showed Peter pieces of clothing the Gazelle had made while she was with them. (Acts 9:39b)

The women held up the garments she had sewn as her creativity—her testimony.

> Peter put the widows all out of the room. He knelt and prayed. Then he spoke directly to the body: "Tabitha, get up." She opened her eyes. When she saw Peter, she sat up. He took her hand and helped her up. Then he called in the believers and widows, and presented her to them alive. When this became known all over Joppa, many put their trust in the Master. (Acts 9:40–42)

Tabitha's vulnerability wasn't in grand speeches or letters from prison but in ordinary acts of creative love. Her blank page was filled with honest whispers of change. Her creativity broke down the walls. And her journey in the wild was resurrected through the miraculous prayer of a fellow wanderer.

John the Baptist brought thunder and wonder, locusts and wild honey. People were drawn from Jerusalem, Judea, and the Jordanian countryside to hear him. The Baptizer preached a simple message: "Change your life. God's kingdom is here" (Matt. 3:2).

When Jesus arrived, John objected to being the one to baptize the One. Yet Jesus insisted. "Do it. God's work, putting things right all these centuries, is coming together right now in this baptism" (Matt. 3:15).

John's creativity wasn't polished. He wasn't smooth around the edges. He wasn't perfect. He wasn't flawless. And he wasn't finished. I can't help but imagine John's entrance to heaven as one with tom drums and melodic guitar riffs. He brought an edge most of us wish we had in our own faith. His creativity was rooted in a simple message and a relentless testimony. He was vulnerable when the Son of Presence was baptized, and the heavens rejoiced as the world was marked with an unwavering love.

No greater love has ever existed.

When I was eight or nine, a Chinese woman unexpectedly arrived at our home in Hong Kong. My parents welcomed her inside, and she sat in our living room. She had been imprisoned in China for her faith and was now free. Her gaze burned with a quiet fire. In her prison cell, she didn't have a Bible: only torn sheets of paper she kept hidden. Scribbled words of Scripture kept her soul alive. As the months passed, she memorized them all. That night in our home, she recited passage after passage from memory.

Her voice remained steady and strong. Vulnerability, confession, imperfection, and testimony made her dangerous to those who attempted to silence her ... and beautiful to those of us listening. Her story wasn't polished, not practiced. It was survival. It was power.

What weaves these lives together is a willingness to bleed truth into culture. To create out of brokenness and strength. Even when unfinished, their testimony cost them, yet allowed their creativity to share truth anyway. In the margins, vulnerability offers us a voice in the wild, and through our creativity, this voice never stops echoing.

Along our journey, we will stand at more than one threshold. We have a choice whether to choose the edge of brave or bury our creativity because we don't feel ready. What if we created it anyway? What would Presence do through us? Crossing this line is never easy. It means leaving the familiar and admitting we don't know all the answers. It means stepping deeper into the margins where nothing is guaranteed.

There will be a cost. But the price has been paid.

For some, the edge of brave is a literal stage, a blank canvas, a boardroom, a pulpit, an open field in a forgotten place. For others, the threshold is an office, a workshop, a classroom, a kitchen table. Wherever our creativity flows onto the page, the truth remains the same. The first step across requires courage, and the second, vulnerability—a passport through the wild as we pursue the whisper and guidance of the Waymaker.

We can't fake it. We can't manufacture it. We can only choose it. One step. Then another. And another. No matter what stands against us. Pierce the noise. Break down the walls. Ignite change. Let courage and creativity flow from our scars with the touch of Presence.

When Paul wrote from prison, he crossed the edge of brave. When Tabitha stitched clothes in obscurity and was brought back to life, she did the same. When John the Baptist baptized the Son of Presence, he knew the cost of following the One would one day lead to the other side—from death to eternity. And when the Chinese woman shared her unpolished story and recited Scripture from memory, her vulnerability was rooted in strength and courage that left a lasting impact.

The margins aren't just a wilderness of risk. They're a place of wild discovery. We bury our wounds in the dirt, and weapons of light pierce through the soil. Creativity invites us to the edge of brave. No more illusions of a flawless masterpiece. In our lives, the margins are marked by scars, silence, rough edges, unfinished chapters. But each one invites us to create it anyway.

> They triumphed over him by the blood of the Lamb and by the word of their testimony; they did not love their lives so much as to shrink from death. (Rev. 12:11 NIV)

Not by polish. Not by perfection. But by their testimony.

Speaking truth, even when it costs—that's the power of vulnerability. It doesn't erase the wound; it heals the calling. In Presence, we are resurrected when shame loses its grip. Isolation shatters. Scars become stories of inspiration. A weapon of light. A testimony.

What we've lived through in the wild isn't just our past; it's our power. The margins are the sacred ground where Presence redeems our pain into purpose and turns our silence into song. Our vulnerable expression means we don't have to wait until our design is perfect, our draft is flawless, our business is thriving, or our healing is complete. We just have to be willing to bleed honesty onto the page and into culture. Someone is waiting to hear our stories, our testimonies, to find courage through our creativity to walk bravely in the wild.

Step up. Speak out. Share honestly. Create it anyway.

9

THE HIDDEN WORK

The Great Western Forum was rocking in game five of the 1991 NBA Finals. A deafening crowd erupted as Michael Jordan and Magic Johnson stepped onto the court. The excitement was electric as two of the best to ever play the game were ready to showcase their creativity. It was hard to believe I was in the arena—the last row of the arena. At the same time, I was conflicted as a Lakers fan and a Jordan follower. (Don't even get me started on the debate about Jordan vs. Kobe vs. Lebron. That's an entirely different conversation best left out of this book.)

The odds were against the purple-and-gold as they faced elimination minus two of their starters, James Worthy and Byron Scott. This didn't stop Magic from scoring sixteen points and adding twenty assists and eleven rebounds to the stat sheet. But Jordan was unstoppable. With thirty points and ten assists, he led the Bulls on a 9–0 run in the fourth quarter to win his first NBA title. This was also the last NBA Finals game to be played in the Forum, and I was there.

Ever since I was young, I've expressed creativity in different ways. More often, I'd be found on a basketball court somewhere. From Kowloon to Los Angeles, the more I worked on my game, the more competitive I became. Whether it was on polished hardwood or cracked asphalt framed by high-rises, I loved putting in the effort to hone my skills.

My fingers spread across a worn ball. The perfect rotation as the grooves slipped from my fingers. The swish of the ball through nylon. It didn't matter if it was a slightly bent rim or in the echo of an arena. My passion for the game started scrappy and grew more creative. If I was going to become a better player, then I had to learn the basics, develop the disciplines of my skills, push myself harder, and focus on ways to beat an opponent.

Friends who know me know this to be true: I never saw a shot I wouldn't take.

To me, the game wasn't only about competition; it was about practicing to showcase my creativity. Angles, rhythms, improvisation. The way a no-look pass felt like writing the perfect sentence. The way a crossover created space like a brushstroke on canvas. There was beauty in the game lived out on the court with a competitive edge.

What captured me about the legends of the game was their relentless pursuit of excellence, their commitment to the disciplines of their skills, and the ways creativity was expressed in the flow of the game. It was never predictable, and it was always captivating.

Now, my first glimpses of my own creativity on the court weren't much to brag about. But the more the mystery of the game focused, the sharper my skills expressed themselves. The more I worked on my game, the better competitor I became on the court. I wasn't afraid to play against anyone, win or lose. And the game offered me something else in return—protection.

Once when I was in junior high in Hong Kong, one of the high school varsity players threw a ball point-blank in my face when I beat him in a game of H-O-R-S-E. While that may not sound like much, it stunned me and rattled my confidence. By the afternoon, the best player on the varsity team found out what happened and stepped in. From that day onward, the best player picked me first anytime we played pickup ball between or after classes.

Not only did his actions protect me, but now I was playing with the best player in the whole school. My game shifted into overdrive because he gave me the confidence to face my bullies head on. Outwork and outhustle. Never back down. On the court, a tenacity was forged in my game, one I have carried with me in life, in calling, and in creativity ever since.

Basketball and creativity share commonalities: Always compete. Always learn. Always pursue greatness. Never allow anyone to stop you from pursuing your creativity. You will never lose if you pour out your best and leave it all on the court.

Like the high-school summer league when I played against a juggernaut who would later be drafted into the NBA. Winning wasn't part of the game plan, as their team was far superior. Still, I wanted to compete, and I accepted the challenge to bring my creativity to the court. He scored thirty or forty points, but I ended up in double-digits, so it was chalked up as more than a victory in obscurity.

In the margins, our pursuit of excellence and purpose is forged in obscurity. Before the applause, the release, the promotion, the accolades, or the game, there is the hidden work. There's the grind no one sees before anyone knows what we're creating or even who we are in this world. It's the midnight rewrites, endless hours in a studio, countless creative sessions, thousands of shots to perfect our rhythm, and routines that build discipline into our creativity. It's the ideas that never make it further than a scribbled page or digital memo. And there are seasons when we step out beyond what's comfortable to discover what's possible—to take our creativity and chase a championship.

For me, one challenge in my creativity was to become an author.

My first attempt at being published ended in bonfire and ash. I'd put myself out there, being vulnerable, and pitched an idea to a publisher. No literary agent. No connections. Just hope and blind belief. But I was a competitor, a gamer, so there was always a chance. Then I caught the attention of an acquisitions editor who showed surprising interest.

The adrenaline spiked when she visited our church to connect with me before one of our services. I believed this might be the break I'd been praying for in the wild. A chance to see a dream realized. When she arrived, I was ready to share my vision for the book and message. To my surprise, she asked me to introduce her to one of our ministry leaders.

She'd come on a different mission. She was playing a different game. One that was misleading. She wanted the celebrity, not the one in obscurity. And I was left burned and a bit jaded. I swore never to do the same to anyone else. But the only way to play was to walk straight into the fire and compete again. That's where excellence and the pursuit of greatness were forged.

As creatives, we will face seasons when we create not because it's profitable or viral but because we're stirred from deep in our soul. In the hidden work, we can't give up after one or two scars. We must welcome relentlessness, courage, and strength to never back down. If Presence has called us to create, then the only choice is how far we are willing to wander in the wild to unearth our creativity.

Are we willing to embrace obscurity to add more color to our canvas? Will we wander with fellow travelers on their unique journey and celebrate their creativity too? That's one piece of the game that always inspired me: playing on a team with others who were all after the same victory.

Far too often, we allow discouragement to consume the hidden work. But Presence has called us to fight using creativity as our weapon. Over the years, I've slayed a few dragons far worse than an acquisitions editor who used me to get to someone else. I could've allowed one moment to stop me from encountering all that Presence had for me. Instead, I kept grinding.

Following *The Disillusioned* book tour, the excitement of meeting new readers, signing autographs, taking selfies, and experiencing the fruit of my labor, I was reminded of that first encounter. There was a sense of satisfaction knowing I'd endured, but my journey was far from over. I still wasn't a bestseller, and the horizon of the stories yet to be written seemed a long way off. Of course, there were moments of discouragement. But I learned something foundational about myself when I stared at another blank page: I thrive in the hidden work, in the discipline to sharpen my skills, even more than the highlight reels.

Yes, there were seasons when I could've been discouraged and given up. But I'd lost games before, and I was willing to compete again. That's what the hidden work requires. Never give up on the calling Presence has prepared in the margins.

Our pursuit of creativity is rooted in diligence and discipline. We can't fully embrace the wilderness seasons unless we are ready to play until the buzzer sounds. In the margins, we become skilled at digging creative ditches in the wild as preparation for the big game. And the hidden work teaches us how to compete and pursue the dreams instilled in us.

What creative seeds are we planting? Are they the right ones? Are we willing to persevere until those seeds sprout? Will we dig deeper to encounter how we might impact culture? Are we willing to sacrifice to experience all that Presence has prepared for us? We can walk through the wilderness of obscurity into seasons of influence. In the hidden work, we have a choice. Win or lose, our creativity shines in the wild.

After *The Disillusioned*, I wrote several spec scripts and another novel. I queried literary agents and searched for opportunities to break through the noise. Along the journey, I was approached to ghostwrite. One was a romance series, which still makes me laugh today considering the genres where I've landed. I even wrote a memoir that was forever shelved after I received a letter from a senator's attorney, who informed me that his relative was arrested and sentenced to prison. I had no idea anything out of the ordinary was happening until the check didn't arrive. You can't make this stuff up.

My dream was to write thrillers, adventures, and edge-of-your-seat page-turners. Instead, romance and memoirs were the storyboards. I thought I was planting pumpkins, but along the way a few cucumber seeds crossed over, and I ended up with mutated pumpcumbers. But these and other books forged the discipline, the routines, the resilience to one day bring characters and worlds to life in my own novels. All the while, the boy between two worlds still spoke to me.

Though I was determined to cultivate the soil, I was left questioning whether I was planting the right seeds. For a season, I needed to stand still in the wild to get my bearings, because I had wandered off course. But I was in survival mode. Any creative knows the tension between the dream and reality. I hustled to keep the lights on, but it wasn't the first time the odds were against me.

I was reminded of the season when I'd risked it all to dive headfirst into building the record company within the church. I'd accepted the challenge knowing the seeds were barely planted. Not only did we gain the respect of the industry and influence in the church, but we also experienced moments when Presence used our creativity to bring others closer to Him. Winning or losing didn't matter in the end. The question was, Did I leave everything on the court?

The same is true in my pursuits as a storyteller. Many were skeptical that I'd ever become an author. And even more were surprised when my creativity landed me producing and directing television. But the unbelief and skepticism only fueled my drive when no one else was watching.

The hidden work is rooted in the grind. There's no way around it. We have to be willing to hone our craft in the margins and the wilderness seasons. In obscurity, our pursuit means the seeds are growing beneath the soil.

During this season, I received an email one afternoon from a major agent in Los Angeles. He'd read *The Disillusioned* and agreed to meet in his office on the Westside the following week. At the time, he also happened to represent one of my all-time favorite bestselling authors. Of course, my adrenaline surged with the opportunity. Maybe this was the big break. Maybe there was a shot at optioning the book for a film. Maybe he'd help me land a big-five publisher, or maybe I'd get to meet the bestseller who inspired my dreams.

Knowing what I know now—not what I believed then—just writing those words makes me laugh. With one email and a phone call, I was convinced I'd won the lottery just because I'd bought a ticket. I'd been in the grind for so long, any shred of hope seemed like salvation.

After nearly three hours on the 405 freeway, which is a parking lot in rush hour, I barely made it on time. Immediately, I was ushered into his office, and for the next hour, we talked about what he enjoyed about the novel and who he represented. This was also the same week my favorite author landed a scripted series deal. Even though it had nothing to do with me, the energy in the room was electric. At the end of the meeting, we agreed that I'd send over a manuscript I'd just finished and go from there.

As soon as I returned home, I fired off the manuscript. One week passed. Then another. More than a month later, I received an email with good and bad news. While the agent responded positively to the story, the challenge was how to break through in the genre. I was still in obscurity, but a few more seeds were tossed and the soil was tilled.

While I loved the creative process of chasing a story, cracking a plot, developing characters, and being lost in these other worlds, a piece of me dreaded the rejection. Each opportunity that reached a dead end left me questioning my creativity. Was it commercial enough? Was I a good enough storyteller? Was I chasing the wrong dream? Was this the calling of Presence?

Every time these thoughts consumed me, Presence reminded me of the day I drove up the 2 freeway and His whisper affirmed what I'd heard on the Zambezi River. This is what I was called to do, so there was no turning back. Win or lose, the hidden work challenged me to keep pushing the limits of my creativity.

Deep down, the challenge is to keep our creativity as the pursuit no matter the roadblocks or mountaintops. Not every team wins a championship every year. Creativity isn't about success as much as it is about exploring and honing our skills. Obscurity is the season when seeds are watered. It's about significance. And in the hidden work is where we find the greatest inspiration.

Culture demands immediate satisfaction, pain free, and overnight success. Creativity is judged by viral moments and billions of views. Success is defined by cash in an account or a cliffside house overlooking a picturesque ocean. A thirst for influence searches for shortcuts in the hidden work to avoid wilderness seasons. We're chasing Michelin Star creativity like we're in a fast-food drive-thru. Sure, we'll get a meal, but it won't be as savory, aromatic, or fulfilling.

In obscurity, the hidden work forges resilience, patience, and endurance. Remember the leader who hid boxes of books in a closet as a fast track to the bestseller list and the record label who altered their numbers to boost their credibility? A desire to proclaim success trumped a desire to dig deeper beneath the soil in the hidden work.

I learned long ago that chasing fame isn't where the hidden work thrives. Through wilderness seasons, I've become more disciplined and passionate about discovering creativity to reach culture. That's what drives me to draw readers into the worlds within the pages. My prayer is to share through story and offer glimpses of the One who inspires my creativity. The grind is challenging, painful, exhausting, and difficult. But the hidden work is pruning, enduring, rewarding, and life-changing.

When seasons of obscurity threaten to leave us in the wilderness dying of thirst, we are reminded who is the River of Life. We no longer chase ghosts—past success or failure—we chase the hidden work in obscurity. When we are beaten down or discouraged, the art of the margins moves us to dig deeper into the soil, because we know the seeds Presence plants will not wither and die.

In the margins, we find the hidden work is oftentimes our most authentic. Not on a stage. Not on a court. Not in front of a crowd. But in the spaces where our creativity pours like a waterfall. That's where our true voice is forged. "But when you pray, go into your room, close the door and pray to your Father, who is unseen. Then your Father, who sees what is done in secret, will reward you" (Matt. 6:6 NIV).

When we show up in secret, we're not creating in vain—we're watering seeds in the soil. We're honing our skills for the championship run. Obscurity isn't exile; it's refinement. It's where growth happens. And if we learn to love the hidden work, we'll carry a resolve and strength that don't depend on being seen by anyone other than Presence. The work we do when no one is watching is the foundation where our creativity unleashes a message to influence culture beyond the game.

That is our reward.

10

WITHOUT LABELS

The roaring cheers caught me off guard. On the other end of the call was my buddy Mitch. He told me to hold on, so I did. Then he rattled off prices in rapid fire, energizing the crowd, which shouted even louder. Each bid jumped by the thousands. In the wife's office, I listened intently, both of us on the edge of our seats.

Mitch is one of the greatest auctioneers to ever step onto the stage. His creative ability to drive bidders higher on the auction block is unmatched. I've seen it with my own eyes: He's poetry in the collector car world. No comparison. And on this day, he was auctioning a green '67 Camaro along with dozens of rare collectibles.

"Fifty thousand. Do you want to bid sixty thousand, D.J. Williams? Traveling the world helping children in the Philippines. Your wife will love it! Sixty thousand ... do you want to bid seventy thousand? Buy it for her! Drive it on the streets of LA! It's only money! Let it bring you happiness today! Write another book or produce a new record!" The '67 Camaro bid climbed with the real bidders until Mitch's voice boomed, "Sold!"

As the crowd roared, Mitch said into the phone, "I'll call you back."

After I hung up the call, the energy from thousands of miles away electrified the room. Another moment passed, and the phone rang again. I answered, "That was awesome!"

We all laughed because I was never bidding!

For nearly thirty years, Mitch's influence in my life has remained steadfast. From the first time we visited the Auburn Cord Duesenberg Automobile Museum until today, he's walked with me through the darkest seasons and celebrated my greatest victories. He's encouraged me along my creative path and listened to my crazy story ideas. He's offered valuable wisdom to guide me in the fog.

We've partnered in creative endeavors and celebrated milestones along the way. We've written books and produced a television series together. We even traveled to Sitio Veterans, where we filmed *The Invitation*. His voice weaved the stories and message together.

Mitch's creativity looks different than mine, and yet we're filled with the same purpose. Some might label him as an auctioneer, and others a biblical scholar. But labels don't capture the impact he's had on my life and the lives of many others. He's been the voice of reason and even an inspiration for my Chase Hardeman series. He's taught me to root my faith deeper beneath the soil and press forward in the wild to create what inspires me.

We've never had to explain our calling to one another, because it's been lived for real, over time. For decades, we've walked together toward who Presence has uniquely called us to be. As wanderers in the wild, we've encouraged one another along the way. We've created what only we could—and let the fruit speak.

No titles needed. Just brotherhood.

We live in a world obsessed with labels: Faith-based. Secular. Sacred. Mainstream. Pastor. Worship leader. Creative director. Artist. Author. Athlete. Producer. Director. CEO. But creativity—real, raw, purposeful creativity—refuses to fit inside tidy boxes. Oftentimes we enjoy the labels because they define us in culture. They define our success. They define our status. They define others' opinions. But what if we chose to create without labels?

Creatives have a hard time with labels because they feel limiting. Labels leave us constrained. We define ourselves within those constraints rather than creating through calling. Labels come with expectation, entitlement, and even envy. We find ourselves wanting what others have, and when those creative pursuits leave us feeling empty, we search for something more to fill the void. In truth, we want to explore, to be free to create and not be confined. We pray for influence to be greater than labels, because creativity speaks for itself. Without labels, we breathe in the wonder of mystery, inspiration, and freedom to exhale our creative expressions.

At times, I've fought against labels: Record exec. COO. GM. Owner. Executive producer. Director. Author. Storyteller. Which one of these defines me the most? Does it even matter? Does choosing between Christian or mainstream entertainment even matter? I've struggled against constraint, because the stories swirling in my imagination appear without limitations. I've come to realize that labels don't define my creativity.

The art of the margins moves us beyond labels and the world's obsession with charisma toward authentic creativity—the character. "Don't be impressed with charisma; look for character" (Matt. 7:16). Some of the most redemptive, culture-shaping work doesn't carry a label. It doesn't need to. When our lives burn with meaning, when our craft flows from a deeper well, creativity carries the fingerprints of Presence. And when we travel with fellow wanderers, labels lose their significance.

Thousands of years ago, the disciples bore the only label that matters: follower of Christ. That was the defining one then, and the same is true today. When we embrace this truth with our whole hearts, we can ignore the other labels and chase Creativity instead. When we stop seeking charisma, whether in ourselves or others, we are free to pursue character. Without any other label, the margins guide us away from what culture defines and leads us deeper toward Creativity, who reflects magnificent wonder.

We are in a culture war where our creativity is a weapon. While some proclaim their faith proudly as influencers, others simply create. We don't always need grand proclamations. We need holy inspirations to reach culture where they are, not where we want them to be. Creativity allows us the space to resonate without being labeled.

> By their fruit you will recognize them. (Matt. 7:16a NIV)

In those moments, we find opportunities to share our faith in the margins of the wild instead of pushing culture aside or preaching to the choir. We're not wired to remain inward. We're called to create outward. We're called to go into all the world, the culture, and share the good news. What form that takes expresses itself through our unique creativity. As much as the world wants to convince us otherwise, there is no formula; there is only freedom.

We've seen throughout Scripture the creative transformation in which those who believed shed the labels for something greater—someone greater—Presence.

Mary Magdalene was an outcast who became a witness. Rahab was a prostitute who became a protector. Peter was a fisherman who became the original Rock. The Samaritan woman was shamed before she was sent. Paul was a persecutor before he became an apostle. Gideon was fearful before he was faithful. All embraced the only significant label: follower of Christ.

Maybe the same is true for you. Labels have defined you for far too long. Your creativity has remained in a tidy box, and maybe now is the time to blow up that box. Allow your creativity to flow like a rushing river through the hands of Presence. Experience the vulnerable transformation in your life and in the unique expressions growing beneath the soil.

Are you willing to journey deeper in the wild to uncover seeds of unlabeled creativity?

You know who you are now, but who might you become?

Each question offers an invitation to walk deeper into the art of the margins.

We are invited to release the pressure to perform our faith and learn to live it through what we create. We can get really good at performing to those around us. We say the right words. We sing the right songs. We quote the right Scriptures. We tithe our 10 percent. We applaud uniquely gifted leaders. We are impressed by charisma in the church and in culture. But the art of the margins calls us to dig deeper to unearth character without labels.

We don't have to brand our calling to be faithful to it. We don't have to label our creations as faith-based, Christian, secular, or anything in between.

Instead, when we create with character, we create in freedom. Presence has instilled in us a weapon to reach the culture for His glory. We don't need permission to be both creative and deeply called. Creativity rooted in the soil of purpose doesn't need the acceptance of culture to grow. We just need to follow character, authenticity, and inspiration so our work, our creativity, our testimony shares a story.

Rather than shouting on a street corner while holding a sign, creatives communicate through story, through canvas, through blueprints, through farm-to-table, through strategy, through products and inventions that shape or revolutionize. When we create rooted in character and without labels, we pivot away from culture defining us. Creativity is soaked in purpose, beauty, passion, and the touch of Presence. And in doing so, we reveal a Kingdom message without ever quoting a verse.

In the margins, we're called to run our own race unlabeled. It may not make sense to others and might even make them a bit uncomfortable. But if Presence is moving us through resistance toward refinement, we will uncover promises of creativity we have not yet seen waiting for us in the wild.

11

ECHOES OF ETERNITY

Cameras rolled as a striking melody echoed over an acoustic rhythm. Within a sanctuary, the lens panned across rows of empty seats before landing onstage. Seated on a stool, Timmons's gravelly voice rang with true conviction in his soul. We were there to capture the moment for *The Invitation* documentary. Though worlds apart, creatives and the children's stories from Sitio Veterans were now uniting in one creative expression.

For sixteen years, Tim Timmons had served as a worship pastor at a megachurch in Southern California. He was known for leading at other churches in the area, as well. That's where we first met. He was a gifted leader, and his craft resonated with large communities. From the outside peering in, he was at the top of his game. And yet he questioned what he was doing.

What did God really care about?

While journaling during this season, he wrote these words: "You're in the preface of the second book of the trilogy of your life."

Sounds like something Gandalf would say!

Timmons and I share a love for *The Lord of the Rings*, and we've both walked through wilderness seasons when we sensed a deeper calling from Presence. For me, this began on the shores of the Zambezi, and for Timmons, the threshold into the margins waited as he began losing favor at the church. He was offered a part-time position or severance, but the questions lingered. If Presence were actually real, was Timmons willing to trust and walk with Him into the wild?

With a wife and four kids, it seemed like an impossible and daunting decision. But there was a sense that more creativity and deeper impact were waiting on the horizon. He asked himself, "What if I quit working for God and just spent time with Him?"

I remember grabbing lunch with Timmons and listening to him share his heart. A few years before, I'd stepped into the unknown and was well aware of the risks and pitfalls in the wilderness. But I was also learning to experience the awe and wonder of Presence walking with me in the margins. Timmons was fighting on more than one front: In 2001, he'd been diagnosed with incurable cancer and given five years to live. Still, his determination to be one whose creativity put good into the world was remarkable and admirable.

We shared our battle scars. We laughed with our unique humor.

As I'm writing this, twenty-five years after that diagnosis, I'm struck by the miracle that Timmons is still on this earth.

Wanderers who have found themselves on the threshold of the margins or in a wilderness season seem to cross my path. Oftentimes my initial reaction in those conversations is to speak truth or resolve the situation with clear steps forward. Whether in the studio, on location, in a boardroom, or exploring with fellow creatives, this is one gift that comes naturally. But in this instance, sitting at lunch with Timmons, I resisted the urge to outline a five-step plan, rattle off techniques, or quote Scripture.

I was simply going to listen. (Yes, miracles do happen.)

My hope was to encourage Timmons, not to steer him along the same path as me but to travel his own path in the wild. In the margins, it's the same wilderness, but each must walk a unique journey. He'd poured out his heart, so I thoughtfully offered lessons I'd learned and those I was still learning about calling, creativity, ministry, and marketplace.

We were both chasing wonder in the wild. I was a few years down the trail, but that didn't mean the questions or answers were any easier. For me, the fellow wanderers who had traveled further ahead brought me the courage to keep walking. I prayed that in the smallest of ways, I'd done the same for him.

Timmons stepped across the threshold into the wilderness and wrote arguably his most profound songs in the unknown. Over the previous eight years, he'd traveled to Nashville at least seven times each year, attempting to open the right doors. But nothing significant had landed. As a creative, it was exhausting to search for ways to schmooze his way in. He was done trying to make it happen, and he asked Presence to open doors for His Kingdom.

Without labels, he put Presence to the test and worked hard at his craft while learning to surrender the outcome. He launched a Kickstarter campaign and raised the budget to produce an indie record with Paul Mabury, two-time Grammy Award–winning musician, producer, and songwriter. The vision for the record was to create art through honest songs.

When the album released, every label in town came knocking. Timmons chose the label who understood his vision, and they struck a deal.

In the margins, he'd stayed grounded and committed in the wilderness. Creativity deepened in the unseen places as he honored the gift, the craft he'd been given. He moved his family to Nashville and pursued his calling as an artist and songwriter. One song in particular, "Even If," was pitched to the label but was passed on shortly before his record deal concluded. While he continued touring, he was left questioning what he was about. He held on to the song, a prayer, as a guarantee to remain committed to working on his craft.

All the while, he had a sense the song was for a friend. Of course, he'd never go to Bart Millard from MercyMe and say, "Hey, I've got this song ..."

One day, Bart and Timmons were in the studio together. Timmons had just had a rough appointment related to his cancer, and he listened as Bart shared about his son's diabetes. Brotherhood was more important than songs or records. To Timmons's surprise, Bart spoke the chorus of "Even If" nearly verbatim, even though he'd never heard the song before. In the quietness of the studio, Timmons played the original song, and together, they worked on what would become the final track. "Even If" would eventually be nominated for a Grammy at the 60th Grammy Awards.

On February 20, 2026, *I Can Only Imagine 2* released in movie theaters worldwide. A sequel to the original blockbuster, the story intertwines with Timmons's life and his song "Even If." What followed for Timmons was a book, *Waking Up Again: A Journey of Grief and Gratitude*. Win or lose, the journey hasn't been about a pursuit of success; it's been about drawing closer to Presence.

Timmons remained faithful to the process, to those he loved in the wild, to the footsteps of Jesus in the wilderness, and to the fruit of walking with Presence. Beyond the songs, the prayers expressed through his creativity and love for people just might be his greatest legacy.

I trudged through the wilderness during the same years as Timmons, long before his story hit the big screen. From one creative endeavor to the next, I hustled, grinded, and pushed harder than ever before—never pausing to reflect on the journey or what was still to come. In the unseen places, I was challenged to sift through every creative idea with a lens of eternity.

What was I creating that would have a lasting impact?

All the while, the boy between worlds grew louder.

A story that might one day become a legacy.

Legacy isn't built in a moment. It's formed in the unseen seasons of faithful creativity. When we step over the threshold into the wild of the margins, we don't know the path ahead. But what we know for certain is we are wandering toward who Presence created us to become. We haven't arrived; we're still arriving. We haven't reached our destination, and still we know eternity is our home. Presence whispers in the wilderness and guides our creativity toward legacy.

Our craft, our art, our calling reflect who Jesus is to culture. In many ways, the church needs to reflect more of Jesus these days. And maybe as creatives, our calling is to allow Presence to speak through our creativity beyond the walls of a church. We may not win Grammys or watch our life story on the big screen, but that should never be the reason.

It wasn't for Timmons.

Again, the most powerful art isn't measured in likes, views, streams, plays, or viral stats—it's measured by legacy. Real impact lingers. It ripples through time, outliving the hands that created it. We may never know who our craft will reach. We may never hear the full story of how a song healed a heart, how a book sparked a breakthrough, how a film entertained and inspired, or how a business became someone's lifeline.

But heaven keeps count.

What we create can echo *for* eternity, but will it echo *of* eternity?

> Let this be written for a future generation, that a people not yet created may praise the LORD. (Ps. 102:18 NIV)

In the margins, we are moved to lift our gaze from the temporary and fix our sights on the eternal. We create as if our craft, our work, matters ... not just now but forever. Creativity resounds in culture through generations in messages of truth, righteousness, peace, faith, salvation, and love. The miraculous power of Presence—of Creativity—breathes the Holy Spirit into our craft and waters our gifts for an eternal purpose.

What we create outlives us. So, what will we leave behind?

Every word, every note, every idea, every unseen impact resonates as legacy.

And what's done in the margins echoes of eternity.

12

TRUST THE TENSION

In the blackness of night, Jacob was alone. He'd left the family safe and now found himself amidst an eerie silence. The stillness didn't last long. A mysterious man appeared, and they wrestled for hours. His muscles burned, his heart pounded, his soul grew weary. And yet he never stopped wrestling. All of the pain, the fear, the doubt poured out as he fought until daybreak.

When the man couldn't get the best of him, he touched Jacob's hip and dislocated it from the joint. Imagine the pain searing through Jacob's worn and exhausted body. All night, he'd kept the upper hand, but with one touch, it was over.

Jacob never gave up. He never let go. He fought with every fiber of his being. And he was left exhausted from the fight. Still, he refused to surrender. He refused to relent. Until the man stopped the all-night battle royale: "The man said, 'Let me go; it's daybreak.' Jacob said, 'I'm not letting you go 'til you bless me'" (Gen. 32:26). A radical request after such a miraculous encounter. Even in his exhaustion, Jacob was willing to wrestle until he received a blessing. Even when it seemed like it was over, he asked for more.

> The man said, "What's your name?" He answered, "Jacob." The man said, "But no longer. Your name is no longer Jacob. From now on it's Israel (God-Wrestler); you've wrestled with God and you've come through." (Gen. 32:27–28)

Jacob wrestled with Presence, the Creator of the universe, and lived to tell the tale. He was blessed for his resilience in the resistance. Have you ever felt like you were wrestling with Presence? With your craft, your creativity, or your unique calling?

I've walked through seasons in the wild when the wrestling was a daily occurrence. Sleepless nights. Days packed with everything other than what I was called to do. Weeks and months wandering in the wilderness digging creative ditches. Long seasons tested my resilience beyond the limits. Surrender wasn't a choice, so I resisted until exhaustion left me on my knees.

I'm wired to work through the chaos, to fight for the next step, to search for solutions, and to be self-sufficient. Many times, I've wrestled for control or to have the upper hand, but the reality is Presence could dislocate my hip at any moment. For me, resistance to surrender is the wrestle. In the margins, I've learned surrender battles against my unbelief, doubt, faithlessness, and self-ambition. But I don't have to wrestle until daybreak; I can simply rest in surrender.

The truth of faith oftentimes mirrors creativity. Resistance wrestles against surrender, yet surrender forges deeper faith. Surrender in the tension strengthens resilience in our creativity. And with the touch of Presence, the blessings flow through our calling.

Every creative knows the hidden tension of the wrestle. The tension between vision and reality where resistance is part of the process. It's the tension in our faith and in our craft that moves us to surrender. Sentences won't land. Chords won't resolve. Keynotes won't capture an audience. Ideas feel just out of reach. Tension in the wild where we wrestle with ourselves, our creativity, instead of surrendering both to Presence.

Do we have the courage of Jacob to wrestle with Presence? To ask Him to bless us?

The wrestle is sacred ground where surrender waits. Exhaustion. Discouragement. Doubt. Dissatisfaction. All of it feels like friction, like failure, like fighting in the dark. We're afraid we're losing, like something isn't working. We question whether our faith is strong enough. So, we wrestle in the margins with Presence ... yet ask for more.

What if we stopped fighting and started trusting the tension?

Tension in the wrestle isn't a sign to quit—it's a sign we're being stretched into who we're becoming. Presence is not afraid of a wrestling match. He welcomes it when we're in the wild pleading for His blessing. He can go on for eternity until we accept that surrender is shaping us into who He created us to be.

Resistance requires us to embrace our calling fully: not partially, not half-heartedly. We won't have the strength to wrestle if we're not fully committed. Instead of fighting against the tension, we should lean into it. That's where transformation takes root. We go from wrestling with Presence to receiving His blessing. Now this doesn't mean the world will spin on our axis. It means that what He has prepared for us will arrive in His perfect time. Growth doesn't happen in the ease ... it happens in the wrestle.

My sophomore novel was a story I loved writing. In it, the kidnapping of an evangelist in the 1920s solves a modern-day mystery. I worked on the manuscript over several years, researching and writing as the story took shape. Late-night creative sessions felt more like wrestling matches as I pushed myself in the tension to hone my craft.

In the end, the novel didn't gain the attention I'd hoped.

Naturally, there was disappointment as I questioned Presence about my calling. I'm a born competitor, so I was still learning to embrace the true meaning of success. Win or lose, I left nothing on the court. Presence reminded me that it wasn't about the sales but rather surrender. That was tough to hear and accept, especially after the effort to bring the story to life. But I chose to bury the dream of turning the novel into a series as one way of surrendering.

Creatives share a graveyard in the wild of creative dreams left as mounds of dirt. Friction in the craft leaves those dreams buried. We can get frustrated when Presence hasn't blessed our efforts. We pray for His direction, but the next blank page seems out of reach. We wrestle with Presence about what's next. But in the friction, something unexpected happens: a touch of creativity.

A fire blazes, and we begin refining our gifts and our craft. Each false start, each blank page, each idea tossed is rooting a resilience beneath the soil. The pressure or disappointment isn't the endgame. In fact, each one proves we're alive, awake, and willing to wrestle for something worth creating. In the margins, we learn to trust the tension as other opportunities present themselves and our craft broadens.

One of the records I produced was tracked at the Firehouse in Pasadena—one of the coolest studios with a warm creative vibe that no longer exists with the evolution away from making records the OG way. On this project, we brought in some of the top musicians in Los Angeles to create around a bonfire. There's something powerful and inspiring about creating in a community of those who bring their pursuit of excellence to share stories through melodies, rhythms, riffs, and harmonies.

We decided to livestream the sessions so others could get an inside look at how the record was made in real time. We broadcast daily as we tracked the songs. We had no idea the response would reach thousands online. That was never our goal. In between takes, we shared stories of the children in Sitio Veterans, and some of the children even joined the livestream, which caught everyone's attention. By the end of the week, we'd finished tracking all the musicians for the record with only an hour to spare in the studio.

On time. On budget. Thank you.

During this creative season, I cowrote more books and even stepped back into the studio to produce for indie artists. But a significant shift occurred when I produced and directed the unscripted television series *The Restoration Road with Mitch Kruse*. Together, we captured incredible, life-changing stories of redemption and restoration. And when the series was syndicated, those stories reached audiences around the world. All the wrestling in the wilderness had broadened my creativity as a storyteller from the page to music to television. The impact of the series was beyond rewarding, but the true gift was walking in the wild together with Mitch.

There is no greater gift or blessing than to sit around the bonfire with fellow wanderers.

While I was grateful for these opportunities, there was still an underlying tension growing beneath the surface between my craft as a storyteller and my calling. I needed to surrender both, again and again. We don't surrender our calling once; we surrender countless times. In the margins, I was learning to surrender my calling and creativity daily. I was reminded stories are shared through music, on the screen, in powerful messages, and on the page.

Still, there was an apprehension to dive into another blank page.

The sting from my second novel left battle scars that flared each time I wrestled with Presence and with my craft. Sparks of inspiration were buried, and my writing paused for a season. Most days, surrender wasn't an easy choice. There was resistance. There was a struggle to trust the tension. The boy between worlds haunted my imagination even though the pages refused to reveal themselves. I'd tested the waters with the idea before and had written drafts, but the blank pages of the full story remained empty. There's no worse feeling as a writer than when the words stop flowing.

> There's more to come: We continue to shout our praise even when we're hemmed in with troubles, because we know how troubles can develop passionate patience in us, and how that patience in turn forges the tempered steel of virtue, keeping us alert for whatever God will do next. In alert expectancy such as this, we're never left feeling shortchanged. Quite the contrary—we can't round up enough containers to hold everything God generously pours into our lives through the Holy Spirit! (Rom. 5:3–5)

In the margins, I was learning to develop patience—which I'm still not great at practicing. But Presence was guiding me to be patient in all things. He was forging and tempering my calling in preparation for what He would do next. Of course, at the time, I didn't know that's what was going on. I was so stuck in a writing slump, I believed it would last forever. At the same time, Presence wasn't shortchanging my calling. The opposite was true: He was stretching me in ways I never imagined ... to strengthen my craft beyond the familiar.

Presence walks with us in the wild, not to leave us wandering but as our guide to show us the way. In our creativity, we might find ourselves creating from unfamiliar places. But the root of our creativity remains the same. If we learn to trust the tension, to surrender, then we are transformed with the strength to pursue our calling wherever it might lead.

It's not always easy, but it is always worth the wrestle.

13

BUILD WHAT'S NOT THERE

The minivan pulled up to the curb outside a nondescript movie theater in the heart of Hollywood. A valet opened the door, and I climbed out of the passenger seat. Strangers waited in line as I stood awkwardly on the sidewalk. I'd been invited by a friend, an Oscar winner, to a private screening of the film *Arrival*.

Before leaving the house, I'd texted and asked about a dress code. His response was, "Casual." While everyone in line was dressed stylishly, I wore a T-shirt and jeans. Of course, in Hollywood it was impossible to know who was who, so I blended in with the artsy crowd.

While the others waited in the cold, I followed my friend through a side door into an empty theater. We had our pick of seats a few rows from the front. I was certain we'd get kicked out at any moment, but I'd had that feeling before and had grown used to being in unfamiliar places. He seemed relaxed, so I tried to act the same. There was definitely a sense I didn't belong, but then again, there was an excitement lingering beneath the surface.

I had no idea who else would be in the theater.

With fewer than seventy seats, the rows filled up quickly. I leaned back in my chair and waited for the film to begin. I noticed two empty chairs onstage directly in front of us. To my surprise, applause erupted in this intimate space as Christopher Nolan and Denis Villeneuve stepped out from the curtains and took their seats onstage.

Immediately, my attention sharpened as two of my favorite directors welcomed us and began a conversation about creativity. Nolan was best known then for the *Dark Knight* franchise and *Inception*, and he would later go on to direct *Oppenheimer*. Villeneuve was recognized for *Sicario* and *Arrival*, and he would later direct the *Dune* franchise. The theater grew silent as Nolan and Villeneuve shared their unique perspectives on filmmaking and their process rooted in the power of story.

Each unique in their approach. Each in pursuit of greatness. Each sacrificed for excellence. Each encouraged the other. Trailblazers with an innate ability to see what others couldn't. Legends climbing toward an Everest summit of their craft. True originals who followed their own path.

Arrival is an amazing film with a stellar cast. After the screening, there was a private gathering, and I was convinced this was the moment when we'd be hauled away. I watched as Nolan and Villeneuve spoke with my friend, an industry legend in his own right. He was decades older than both of them, but when they realized who he was, their brows raised and the conversation continued with a level of respect for a fellow trailblazer. I was honored to shake the hands of greatness, then ride home in my friend's minivan.

Even for one night, being in the presence of such legendary filmmakers brought a sense of wonder. Not because they were in the industry, but because of the respect and commitment they held for their craft. They didn't take their creativity for granted, and they didn't follow the status quo. I was inspired to take another step in the wild to push the limits of my creativity.

I may never reach the heights of the legends, but that isn't the endgame. In my own way, in the way Presence uniquely created me, witnessing greatness inspired me to risk more than I thought possible. And I'm still challenged to pursue the stories that resonate in my soul and to commit to seeing those original creations through to the end.

The world doesn't need more replicas. There is a tendency to imitate success and expect to experience the same fulfillment as the originals. But Presence isn't calling us to be imitators; He's calling us to be innovators. He's calling us to be original, to be pioneers in our art, our craft, as we climb toward the summit of our unique calling.

We're not called to copy anyone else, because Presence has engrained originality into our soul. When we chase the creativity of others, we're simply running in the opposite direction of our wilderness journey. For some, the most impactful work we'll ever create won't have a road map. No manual. No mentor. Just a whisper from Presence deep in our spirit that says, *Go*.

That's how sacred creativity begins.

That's how we create and build what's not there.

Builders, inventors, filmmakers, artists, writers, and visionaries are rarely handed permission slips. Instead, we're handed resistance. Doubt. Delay. Destruction. When we're called to create what doesn't exist, the absence of precedent isn't a barrier—it's confirmation. It means we've been entrusted with an original. And we were created not to follow a path but to make one.

Creatives see what others don't; we're trailblazers. We're the ones who chase the tornadoes of the unknown. We're the ones with blueprints burned into our souls, waiting for the courage to draw the first line. We may not have a map, but we have a mission. So, we build and create anyway.

Peter Jackson brought *The Lord of the Rings* from the page to the screen in an epic, nearly impossible saga. He changed the future of filmmaking forever. As I said, the director's cut of the trilogy and behind-the-scenes footage of the creative geniuses who brought Middle-earth to life is unmatched. The sheer scope of the production required the evolution of Wētā Workshop to make the impossible possible through groundbreaking digital and practical effects.

If you've never watched the behind-the-scenes, you're missing out on a master class of creatives showcasing their skills. The original works of J. R. R. Tolkien, the writers of the screenplays, incredible cast, producers, composer, cinematographer, editors, orchestra, production designer and team, art directors, set directors, makeup department, production management, second unit directors, assistant directors, art department, sound department, special effects, visual effects, stunts, camera and electrical department, casting, costume and wardrobe, editorial, location management, music department, script and continuity department, transportation department, and additional crew.

You might be wondering why I've listed each one. It's simple: Every person who was involved in the production brought their unique creativity for a massive vision around a bonfire in the wild. And they built what wasn't there, what had seemed beyond their reach.

One of my favorite behind-the-scenes moments was when Peter Jackson was in a London hotel finishing one script, approving scenes on another screen, while watching a live orchestra recording an epic soundtrack. His vision burned in his soul and refused to relent. He pushed himself beyond the limits, because his commitment was unwavering.

We can learn from the greats like Nolan, Villeneuve, and Jackson about the discipline and sacrifice required in our creative work. And this isn't limited to filmmakers. We've seen this throughout history whenever originals built what was not there. Instead of following a familiar path, they made their own.

Born into slavery, George Washington Carver was an agricultural scientist who became the most prominent Black scientist of the early twentieth century. His ingenuity and knowledge observed solutions in the soil no one else did by altering the planting of cotton and crops including sweet potatoes and legumes, like peanuts and soybeans. He created a future in the environment, which revolutionized agriculture.

Most have heard the story of how Steve Jobs started Apple in his garage. He faced the tornadoes of adversity, setbacks, ridicule, competition, and failure along an unseen path. He was even fired from the company he founded. For years, he was a refugee of Apple ... until he returned with a sharper creative vision that revolutionized industries and forever changed culture.

Bob Dylan's songs were prophetic cultural anthems. From "The Times They Are a-Changin'" to "Blowin' in the Wind," his artistry disrupted, provoked, and called forth societal change. With an estimated one hundred million records sold worldwide, Dylan has received an Academy Award, ten Grammy Awards, Kennedy Center Honors, a National Medal of Arts, the Presidential Medal of Freedom, induction into the Rock and Roll Hall of Fame and the Songwriters Hall of Fame, and even been awarded a Nobel Prize in Literature. Dylan charted his own path, one for the history books.

Nick Vujicic was born with tetra-amelia syndrome. With the absence of arms or legs, he was bullied at school. He attempted suicide. But when he turned seventeen, his creativity brought him to inspirational speaking and later to becoming an author. His life and message have reached millions around the world. He's a pioneer, an original who has conquered obstacles with a resounding faith that inspires others from all walks of life.

Each one is a trailblazer in their own creativity. While they may not share the same faith, their relentless ability to build what others could not unites them around the bonfire of creatives. We may never reach the same legendary status, but we are called to pursue our calling with an equal resilience, determination, and belief.

We may not find ourselves on a film set directing a superhero movie or on a stage, welcoming the applause of thousands. We may never experience our songs reaching a million streams. We may never build a company that literally alters culture. But then again, we just might one day. In the margins, we are called to see what others don't and build what's not there. And for those of us who believe, we are given one of the greatest gifts—faith and trust in Presence along our journey.

Hebrews reminds us:

> The fundamental fact of existence is that this trust in God, this faith, is the firm foundation under everything that makes life worth living. It's our handle on what we can't see. The act of faith is what distinguished our ancestors, set them above the crowd. (Heb. 11:1–2)

The art of the margins calls us to disrupt, provoke, and bring forth change in culture. We too are the trailblazers. We are the ones who chase the tornadoes of the unknown. We are the ones with blueprints burned into our souls, searching for the courage to draw the first line. We may not have a map, but we have a mission, a calling. We weren't made to follow someone else's path. We were created to follow in the footsteps of Presence. If we embrace the impossible in faith and trust, our calling will burn like a raging inferno as we carry our weapon of creativity into battle.

In the words of Gandalf the Grey:

> All we have to decide is what to do with the time that is given to us. There are other forces at work in this world, Frodo, besides the will of evil.[4]

14

WHEN THE SPARK FADES

Explosions thundered in the night as a woman carried a lamp of light amidst the suffering. Soldiers wounded in battle, some on the verge of the other side, desperate to be saved. This woman remained quietly persistent. She understood suffering and was willing to fight the battle on her own terms. Florence Nightingale was a British nurse during the Crimean War. But she wasn't just any nurse: She was on the forefront of revolutionizing nursing in field hospitals. Her creativity allowed her to significantly reduce soldier mortality by reforming sanitary conditions, which saved countless lives.

The thunder raged, war erupted, and casualties mounted.

Nightingale carried hope for the suffering with a lamp of light.

There will be seasons when we feel like we've gone to war and ended up on a stretcher when the spark fades. Our gifts aren't flowing through our veins like they once did. We feel a sense of suffering because what we were created to do isn't happening. The gifts within us seem to be on life support. But there is light in the battle, even if it's hard to find.

Every creative knows the drift. A fire that once burned hot begins to flicker. We stare at the same screen, the same canvas, the same dream—and it feels like we're losing the war. A spark that once lit up our soul now barely flickers. We're lost in the in-between. Days when isolation is quiet. When the craft feels more like discipline than pleasure. When the scars are open wounds that leave us flat on our backs gasping for new life. These are not wasted moments; they're the proving ground of our purpose, our resolve, our resilience.

In the wars of the wild, we don't create just when it's easy; we show up when it's dry, when it's slow, when the world and life crash into us, and when we're suffering in silence.

Imagine the soldiers during the Crimean War who fought the enemy and landed in a field hospital. The despair, the pain, the agony, the loss. When it seemed as if their life was over, a nurse passed by with a lamp of light. A flicker of hope they wouldn't die. Night after night, Nightingale used her gifts to rescue, restore, and redeem.

For long seasons, I've fought my own wars in the wild and cultivated creative ditches in the wilderness. You see, creativity isn't constant—it's cultivated, and we must fight for it. I'd stand before each ditch with shovel in hand and plant seeds of the stories I hoped to one day write. While keeping my head down, I dug more ditches, planted more seeds, then covered each one with hope and prayer.

In the darkness, I fought discouragement, disillusionment, and doubt. Even though I was tempted to look up and gaze at others around me, the grind and hustle kept me grounded. One episode at a time. One creative project at a time. One blank page at a time. No glory. No fame. Just the craft. And a belief that one day the harvest would come.

I realized the outpouring of my creativity reflected seasons of faith and trust. Not that it was easy. It was hard to surrender to the unknown. There were times when my belief was strong and other times when I questioned Presence. I'd been raised in the church, so you'd think my faith would be unshakable. But there were moments when the ground shook beneath me. So, I did what I knew to do: I shoveled ditches in the wild from sunrise to sunset, believing for a new season.

I thought about Mom. The years she battled against her own struggles, yet her faith in Presence remained steadfast. She didn't give up, no matter how the church or the world defined her challenges. No matter where my journey might lead, I was determined not to give up either. Maybe it was my way to honor her fight. Maybe it was a reminder of the Sunday morning in the back row when I accepted Presence into my life at eight years old. Maybe it was a belief that the art of the margins was shaping me to be stronger.

I was learning to carry a lamp of light in the wild. I did my best to cultivate the creative ditches and water the seeds. Beneath the soil, roots took hold, and my creativity was expressed in other ways: hundreds of episodes of television, creative endeavors, and production that kept my dream alive. All of it was challenging, motivating, inspiring, and satisfying because of the vision for each one and the community who surrounded the bonfires.

It wasn't like I was lost or alone in the wilderness. It's just there were creative ditches of my own where the roots had yet to break through. Whenever I turned toward the light to go deeper in faith and trust, the roots grew a bit more. But when my faith was dormant, so were the roots. I prayed for Presence to guide me toward the harvest, but patience was still the wrestle.

During this season, I had an opportunity to watch a prerelease of *The Last Jedi* on the Walt Disney Studios lot. I'd grown up with all of the action figures from the original *Star Wars* saga. While most gravitated toward Luke Skywalker, my attention turned toward Han Solo. Something about Solo has always resonated with me. He was an outlier, and I'm the same.

Walking on the Disney lot was a surreal experience. To think that Walt Disney, another outlier and one of the most imaginative visionaries in entertainment, dug his creative ditches and watched those worlds grow in this place and beyond. But Disney faced setbacks, failures, the bankruptcy of his first animation studio, and countless rejections. His journey in the wild wasn't a rocket-ship ride on Space Mountain. Yet he persevered to witness his vision become reality and in the process built a global media and theme park empire.

Disney's relentlessness was rooted in a vision. Cultivating that dream required endurance, and nothing less. And it required faith and trust even when the spark faded.

I can't help but think of heroes in the Bible who faithfully cultivated and endured in the wild. Joseph was sold into slavery by his brothers, then accused and imprisoned for a crime he didn't commit. Still, his loyalty remained steadfast as he stayed close to the light. Presence had a plan for his life that was revealed in time, and his faith saved nations (see Gen. 37, 39–50).

And there's Hannah, who diligently prayed for a child. She promised to dedicate her son if Presence answered her prayers. When she gave birth to Samuel, her faithfulness and endurance brought to this world a great prophet who would go on to anoint two kings of Israel. She was a living witness of how persistent cultivation leads to answered prayers and deeper faith (see 1 Sam. 1–2).

We can't go on without wandering for a moment with Job. He lost everything, yet his faith remained steadfast. His faithfulness was a battle amidst immense suffering. Just to survive took courage and a resilient belief in Presence. And it was the lamp of light shining in the midst of his suffering that brought restoration (see the book of Job).

> So let's not allow ourselves to get fatigued doing good. At the right time we will harvest a good crop if we don't give up, or quit. Right now, therefore, every time we get the chance, let us work for the benefit of all, starting with the people closest to us in the community of faith. (Gal. 6:9–10)

The art of the margins teaches us that in the worn edges of our creativity, trust leads to endurance, endurance leads to faithfulness, and faithfulness leads to breakthrough. While we might feel isolated in the wilderness, our calling and craft continue to show up in the silence. Our work of creating is rooted in a belief it will be worth it all and our craft will ultimately honor Presence. We will have to choose whether we are willing to risk, to be patient, to endure hard seasons to experience the harvest. And if we cultivate our faith and our craft, then Presence will honor us.

One of the greatest examples of faithfulness in the fire is Shadrach, Meshach, and Abednego, who defied King Nebuchadnezzar (see Daniel 3). Because they refused to bow down to worship the Babylonian king, the three men were thrown into a fiery furnace to be torched alive. Miraculously, the king witnessed a fourth man appear in the inferno—the Son of Presence. Even in the face of death, their faithfulness brought a king to acknowledge Presence as the one true God. And when they stepped out from the flames, they were blessed with higher positions in Babylon.

When the spark fades, keep showing up. Faithfulness unleashes a holy fire. Not for a select few, but for all who believe. Don't give up. Don't quit. Trust.

Believe. Endure. Dedicate your craft to Presence. That changes everything when the spark fades. You won't create for glory ... you'll create for His grace. You won't accept your obscurity, because you are already known. Surrender your creativity in faith, and you will find freedom in the harvest.

While the tale of Shadrach, Meshach, and Abednego is a miraculous story, faithfulness is not flashy: It's firewood. Stack it daily, and one day—when we least expect it—the spark will catch again. And this time, it'll burn deeper, brighter, stronger. Because the fire that survives the silence, the doubt, the struggle will endure forever and shape who we become.

In the wild, I built a fire around my creative ditches and mounds of fresh soil. I wasn't alone in the blaze of life. Presence was with me from sunrise to sundown. Around the bonfire, orange embers drifted in the night as a renewed faith burned in my soul. Late nights were spent staring at the blank page and exploring my craft. Night after night, the blank page stared back, daring me to go deeper. I chose to endure in the unknown, not searching for my glory but for His grace. A renewed fire burned in faithfulness as a harvest broke through the soil.

15

SACRED RESISTANCE

A stench permeated the air of a damp prison where the guilty and innocent were locked away. Among them were Paul and Silas. Both were flogged, beaten, and thrown in a cell. Think about that for a moment. Flogged. Beaten. Prison. Not writer's block. Not a struggle with color on canvas. Not a canceled artist tour. Not a business deal gone south. The stakes were higher than most of us will ever experience in our lifetime. Still, Paul and Silas were not helpless.

Real life. Gritty faith. Unrelenting calling.

Paul and Silas were followers of Jesus who pursued calling over self, both willing to suffer in the name of Christ. Their crime? Paul had commanded an evil spirit to leave a slave girl. The miracle of freedom for her landed Paul and Silas in prison, and darkness surrounded them. Guards were fearful the new prisoners might escape, so they clamped their legs in irons. Makes you wonder if perhaps the Jesus story of miracles, crucifixion, and resurrection had reached this city, since no jailer or guard wanted to lose another body.

Yes, Jesus rose from the dead. Now Paul and Silas were facing death. So, what did they do when the odds were against them? They prayed and sang loud enough for the other prisoners to take notice. The raw power of faith and worship blended as gifts of creativity poured out. Scripture says the prisoners couldn't believe their ears. Imagine a host of angels singing along with them.

Right around midnight, a massive earthquake shook the prison so violently the cell doors flew open. As a Californian, I'm well aware of the rattle and roll. All the prisoners were loose. A massive jailbreak was inevitable. But then something unforeseen occurred: No one left.

> The jailer got a torch and ran inside. Badly shaken, he collapsed in front of Paul and Silas. He led them out of the jail and asked, "Sirs, what do I have to do to be saved, to really live?" They said, "Put your entire trust in the Master Jesus.

> Then you'll live as you were meant to live—and everyone in your house included!" (Acts 16:29–31)

In the early hours, the jailer and his whole family were baptized. When the local judges realized that Paul and Silas were Roman citizens who had done nothing wrong, fear moved them to set both free. If we played out this scene a few more beats, we could see their decision was a direct result of prayer and worship so powerful that it shook the prison to its foundation.

I love what happened next: Paul and Silas didn't hightail it out of town, as the local officials hoped they would. Instead, Paul refused to back down. He put the judges in their place until they apologized and personally escorted them out of the jail.

Relentless conviction. A sacred resistance.

Paul stood his ground rooted in faith. Some might conclude this means that when we put our trust in Jesus and live as we were meant to live, we'll never face tribulation. Others might believe such miracles are only for those who are spiritual giants—the ones who can survive and conquer the worst of humanity and the most evil in the spiritual realms. But conviction and sacred resistance are for all who believe, including you and me. We are in a battle for souls, and the warrior's cry proclaims our trust in Jesus, who walks with us into the dungeons as a sacred resistance is forged.

In the margins, faith is calling, calling is worship, worship is warfare, and creativity is our weapon. If we fully surrender ourselves, that doesn't mean we are more spiritual than others. None of us has lived a perfect life. All have fallen short. If someone tells you differently, then a mirror is in their future. The question is: Are we willing to go deeper in our faith if it means enduring suffering? Are we willing to pursue our calling, our creativity, our craft if there is a price? Naturally, we don't welcome seasons of struggle or suffering. But followers of Christ, believers in Presence, who wander deeper into the wild embrace this calling and accept the cost.

How do we endure? Like Paul and Silas, we choose a sacred resistance.

The art of the margins forges this resistance in our souls. We refuse to give up, to give in, to give ourselves to anything apart from the will of Presence. Flowery words are not enough. Hiding in the comfort of our church, studio, office, and home will not protect us. We cannot hide behind our gifts, our craft, our success, or our failure. When the war rages and the enemy strikes, a sacred resistance in the trenches is what will pull us through.

Sacred resistance is where a holy toughness is forged.

In our calling and creativity, these seasons of endurance guide us through the wilderness. After the ground shakes, we walk wiser, stronger, and even more committed to pursue Presence above all else. We don't face resistance when the stakes are small. We face resistance when we've stepped into the sacredness of the wild. Resistance isn't a sign we're failing; it's a sign our work carries eternal weight. In the moments we begin to build what matters—when creativity aligns with calling—expect pushback, expect friction, expect iron clamps on our craft and our gifts, expect invisible forces to build strongholds against us charging forward in battle.

> God is strong, and he wants you strong. So take everything the Master has set out for you, well-made weapons of the best materials. And put them to use so you will be able to stand up to everything the Devil throws your way. This is no weekend war that we'll walk away from and forget about in a couple of hours. This is for keeps, a life-or-death fight to the finish against the Devil and all his angels. (Eph. 6:10–12)

We fight not against flesh and bone. Worship is our battle cry in the war. Creativity is our weapon in the fight. Testimony shines a light on eternity. Sacred resistance conquers all darkness.

Spiritual opposition confirms spiritual assignment. Resistance validates calling. If we're facing a tough season in the margins, then we're on the verge of a breakthrough. But we're going to have to fight in the suffering. We see throughout the Bible and in history how followers of Christ, believers in Presence, weren't only singing "Hallelujah"; they were also risking their lives and wielding their weapons to defend and share the greatest story ever told.

Bono is one who has used his creativity to fight against extreme poverty, HIV/AIDS, malaria, and human-rights abuses, and he cofounded organizations like ONE and (RED). He's also been more outspoken in recent years about his faith and reluctance toward the institution. I believe he's been on a spiritual assignment that has garnered the attention of culture and the Church.

Yes, he's controversial at times. But maybe that's part of the sacred resistance too.

Since the early eighties, I've been on the U2 bandwagon, even when the tension between their music and the Church was strong. In many ways, it made me want to listen to more of their songs. Today's worship leaders and songwriters can thank Bono, the Edge, Adam, and Larry for inspiring the sound of modern worship. Maybe Bono's sacred resistance is because he carries a relentless conviction. Maybe spiritual opposition confirmed spiritual assignment.

I was one of nearly one hundred thousand fans packed into the Rose Bowl in Pasadena when the U2 360° Tour came to town. From the first note, the entire stadium sang along to every hit. Always pushing the edge, the visuals captivated and communicated the messages and causes close to Bono's heart. While the entire concert was incredible, one moment toward the end stood out to me more than any other—when "Amazing Grace" segued to "Where the Streets Have No Name." You're probably humming the melody right now.

With only Bono's signature vocals and his guitar, the crowd sang along: "Amazing grace, how sweet the sound, that saved a wretch like me! I once was lost, but now am found, was blind, but now I see." And when the Edge came in with the iconic wall of sound leading into "Where the Streets Have No

Name," there was a breaking free beyond entertainment. The bravery of the fight, the boldness of worship, and the unabashed testimony were in harmony with Presence.

When the concert was over, there was a buzz. Even as we headed for our cars, the crowd was still singing. Of course, the night wasn't over. Because of the almost one hundred thousand people, it took us nearly four hours to get home, even though it was only twelve miles away. But every second in traffic was worth the encounter.

Culture pushes back on our fight, our worship, our testimony, refusing to accept bold creativity in the name of Presence. Bono and U2 are exceptions, as they've shaped culture over decades. For a long time, creativity in sharing the gospel message was not at an equal level of excellence as compared to the culture's expressions. Oftentimes it was ten strides behind in the battle. But that tide is shifting. I believe it's because creatives are embracing a sacred resistance to the culture through a holy toughness.

Bravery is at the tip of the spear for creatives who battle darkness in the wild. Presence promises to walk with us when evil comes to steal and destroy. A sacred resistance moves us to our knees in worship, to call out to Him and wield our creativity for His glory. Not every war is visible. Some of the fiercest battles happen in the soul. In the spiritual realm, creativity is a mighty weapon against discouragement, delay, insecurity, and distraction.

The greater the purpose, the greater the resistance to derail destiny. We were never meant to create from comfort. We were called to create from conviction. The ground we're standing on might be contested, but it's also consecrated. If our work stirs something holy, it will be challenged. And that's not a sign to retreat—it's a moment to dig in, it's our chance to fight, it's a promise to rise.

16

WORK BEFORE THE WORK

A jet careening toward the earth. A father. A son. An auctioneer. A highly skilled operative from the shadows. That was the beginning of a new story I'd been preparing to write for a long time. While it wasn't the boy between worlds, it was where I found my sweet spot. It was where my voice as a storyteller felt the most natural.

For months, I wrote from 9 p.m. to midnight. The blank pages filled up like never before. Chapters flowed, and characters breathed. Without a grand platform, it was the fruit of the work before the work. Years of preparation as a storyteller taught me to keep a posture of faithfulness in the process. I trusted the tension even when the odds were stacked against me.

Everyone wants the moment. Few are willing to live through the preparation that makes the moment possible. There's a holy grind that happens when no one is watching. The grind lasted for years before I wrote the first line of *The Auctioneer*. By then, I'd produced and directed television and pitched a list of show concepts to the networks and studios. I'd even partnered with other creatives with a major brand and production company owned by one of the most successful reality show executive producers of all time. Still, I returned to this story.

Maybe the preparation was prophetic. Maybe I was always going to write this thriller. Maybe I was going to deliver a bestseller. So much remained unanswered until the story was finished. Until then, I captured the world in my mind. Until then, I chased the characters wherever they led. Until then, the blank pages were no longer blank.

Those late nights were filled with dreams, visions, voices, and scenes playing out in my imagination. The writing process slowly shifted from a grind to a front-row seat. How did this happen? Before the stage, before the release, before the launch, before the breakthrough ... there's repetition in the silence. The hidden, sacred work that shapes who we are when the lights turn on. Each night, my creativity ran wild. Night after night. Week after week. Month after month. There was a rhythm to my writing that created an undeniable momentum on the page.

I didn't have the luxury to drop all of the other projects to chase one story. Still, discipline in the sacred resistance and determination to cross the finish line kept me watering the soil. We often underestimate the power of the unseen. In the Kingdom, preparation in the wilderness seasons strengthens our calling. Presence doesn't waste the private grind. He uses it to forge the voice, the vision, the resilience we'll need when the weight of our calling gets real.

The work before the work is a call to discipline before display. Discipline is an art unto itself. Despite what many believe, discipline is not restricting. Rather, it strengthens our craft so we can have freedom in our creativity. We're reminded how showing up when no one sees plants seeds of greatness that need cultivating. What we're building in secret will one day have a voice in the world—if we don't quit in the quiet.

Musicians who spend hours practicing chords and scales. Producers and directors who map out every scene on storyboards. Entrepreneurs who run through pitches a hundred times while developing steps for product success. Those in ministry who faithfully commit to being in the Word, diligently shepherding and serving their community.

Discipline fuels our passion and forges our gifts in holy fire.

Thousands of years ago, David was a young shepherd boy who tended to his father's sheep. In fields far from royalty, he remained committed to the mundane. Even after he was anointed by Samuel to become the next king, he found himself still out with the flock singing songs no one ever heard and slinging rocks in the wild.

King Saul was losing his mind, and David was brought to him as a comfort. Those songs from the field became soothing melodies for a king who lost favor with Presence. David's discipline to serve and to sing prepared him for a prophecy on the verge of coming true. David versus Goliath. One stone killed a giant. One victory changed a nation.

But instead of being hailed a hero, David became a fugitive. He witnessed Saul's jealousy seeping deeper into the king's bones, leaving his victory against the Philistine short-lived. From the caves, David became a warrior who fought bravely, courageously, and valiantly. He led an army willing to die in their loyalty to him. He was a king without a crown. He was faithful in the small things, and Presence honored him with favor when he became the king over Israel.

> If you're honest in small things,
> you'll be honest in big things;
> If you're a crook in small things,
> You'll be a crook in big things.
> If you're not honest in small jobs,
> who will put you in charge of the store?
> No worker can serve two bosses:
> He'll either hate the first and love the second
> Or adore the first and despise the second.
> You can't serve both God and the Bank. (Luke 16:10–13)

One of my friends, Jaime Jo Wright, happens to be a bestselling author. We share a wicked sense of humor, which makes our conversations slightly unpredictable. She's a fellow creative who's walked through seasons in the wilderness, and she's a prolific writer. I'm like Wile E. Coyote, and she's like Road Runner. Every time we connect, she's finishing another book. She understands the life of a creative as well as anyone. And she understands the value of the work before the work.

Jaime dove in headfirst with a historical romance suspense novel. She submitted her manuscript at a time when the industry was nose-diving. None of the publishing houses were buying. During this season, a well-established author who mentored her offered some sage advice: Why don't you write dual-timeline fiction where past, present, and mystery collide? At the time, she didn't know what kind of genre this was, but she was intrigued.

She began to see elements of creativity as puzzle pieces needing to be fitted together. With nothing to lose and a posture of faithfulness, she dreamed up a concept about an old, abandoned house. What if the walls could talk? She sensed her creativity shift, and slowly, she returned to what she loved. She had tried to adapt to the industry market, but this time, she turned the tables and wrote what was burning in her soul. Discipline in the unseen, exploring as part of her process, strengthened her creativity and pulled her closer to her true calling.

The House on Foster Hill launched Jaime's career.

Awards and accolades followed.

In seasons when she was overlooked, faithfulness and discipline fueled her creativity. Early on, when she had queried a potential literary agent, she received a scathing response: "You have written the worst hero ever, I was so bored." For most creatives, these can be dark moments. Rejection always feels personal. But it's one person's opinion. Still, we find those opinions stick with us longer than the ones that are positive and encouraging. Those disheartening words play over and over.

What if we approached those moments like David did? Yes, we're frustrated or angry. Still, we will continue to sing, to write, to lead, to serve, to build. Those moments do not define us. We don't know when our breakthrough will happen, so we must hold on to a posture of faithfulness in the storm.

When Jaime sent the same manuscript and proposal to another agent, she received this response: "Dear Jaime, you have written probably one of the most memorable heroes I have ever read in fiction." Boom! This agent signed Jaime and sold *The House on Foster Hill.*

We don't need a platform to prepare. In obscurity, the work before the work is the preparation. Faithfulness is the cornerstone of our mission, our calling. Discipline in our craft might seem mundane … until we kill Goliath.

Without a posture of faithfulness, we find ourselves lost in a wilderness of comparison. The more we compare ourselves to others, the less we're creating.

And when we face rejection, those comparisons paralyze our creativity. In the margins, we realize the question that is most grounding isn't, "Presence, can I get there too?" but "Presence, will You protect me on my journey, which is unique from theirs?" Presence promises to give us the desires of our hearts—which is not a laundry list of wants and needs. Our greatest desire must be to seek Presence and grow close to Him. That's all that matters.

The good news is there is no risk of rejection when we reach out to Presence in the wild. When we pursue the heart of Creativity, we follow where He leads. We stop worrying about acceptance or rejection, and we focus on the Goliath charging toward us. When we embrace this truth as our greatest desire, our creativity will go places we never imagined.

In the preparation, the work before the work, in the small things, the disciplines in our craft, there is faith and hope. Our creativity goes from black and white to vibrant color. And the story of our epic journey shifts in the realms of heaven.

We are seen. We are warriors. We are rock slingers.

One of my favorite streaming series is *House of David*. It not only follows David's story but visualizes it in a cinematic world rivaling the best of entertainment. And more importantly, it has accomplished this with a level of humility that is admirable. In a culture that praises celebrity, whether in the church or in the mainstream, this is refreshing.

Many have a picture of Hollywood as the place to be discovered, to be seen, and where dreams come true. While this is reality for some, it is oftentimes temporary. Fame in this world is fleeting. We were seen by Presence before we were conceived—before we were in our mother's womb. We've been created by the most magnificent being of creativity in the universe: Presence. The value in who we are is not in what we do but in who we are in Him. We don't need a platform or fame to be used by Presence ... we need a posture of humble faithfulness.

In the margins, our value is being seen and shaped by Presence. The work before the work forges in us the discipline to keep our eyes and hearts focused on this truth. We can't run on the hamster wheel of self-ambition forever. Someone else will always run faster and harder. But if we look to be seen by Presence, then we learn to truly see Him. Everything else fades away except the certainty of who He is and who He has called us to be. That's all the fame we need.

David was a shepherd boy who became king.

Jaime was a dreamer who became a bestseller.

Me—I was on my own journey of faithfulness, and it all started with a plane crash.

17

LEAD WITH WONDER

Butterflies ravaged my nerves as I stepped onto the stage of a packed room. My heart pounded as my fingers gripped the lectern tightly. Steadying myself, I exhaled slowly and gazed across the audience. In those few seconds of quiet, fear and anxiety crashed into adrenaline and focus. A lifelong struggle with public speaking threatened to paralyze me—then it faded.

Months earlier, I was invited to be a keynote speaker at a writers' conference in Colorado. I'd never thought of myself as a public speaker. I'd spent the majority of my career behind the scenes and camera, in editing rooms, in studios, in forgotten places of the world, and writing every night until midnight. Since I was young, I'd avoided the spotlight unless it was on a basketball court. Two different arenas, one fearful of an audience and the other feeding off the crowd when the game was on the line. Still, I was curious.

Leading up to the conference, I had been in the process of writing *The Auctioneer*. At the time, I didn't know how this novel would change the trajectory of my storytelling. The first book in the Chase Hardeman series was inspired in part by my friend Mitch and my love for espionage thrillers. In the opening pages, a jet crash unlocks a world and characters I've grown to love. I was still a few years away from the actual release, but I knew I'd found where I belonged.

Fast-forward several years and *The Auctioneer* ranked alongside some of my favorite authors climbing the lists on Amazon. While it wasn't a *New York Times* bestseller, it was a breakthrough. After years of grinding, hustling, and chasing a dream, there was satisfaction. It was a reminder of what really matters in the margins. We're not called to outperform our past; we're called to out-trust our fear. I was still learning success wasn't the endgame—the endgame was significance and closeness to Presence.

You blew with all your might
and the sea covered them.

They sank like a lead weight
in the majestic waters.
Who compares with you
among gods, O God?
Who compares with you in power,
in holy majesty,
in awesome praises,
wonder-working God? (Ex. 15:10–11)

Chase success as an endgame, and we're left feeling empty after we cross the finish line. Search for ambition apart from Presence, and we're left wanting more to fill the void. Pursue significance, and a righteous weight of legacy guides us. Wander after the awe of Presence, and freedom lights our creative way. To create boldly. To share truth. To lead with wonder.

When seeds grow into vines breaking through the soil, there is a temptation to pump the brakes and wait at the threshold. We question whether we are ready … or worthy. We spend seasons in the wilderness in preparation, and still we pause when the edge of brave calls us deeper. We are afraid to create. We are afraid to share our testimony. We are afraid to lead with wonder—and to lead others *toward* wonder.

Rewind the timeline.

Dread seeped beneath my skin when I landed in Colorado for the writers' conference. In that moment, I second-guessed my decision. My curiosity had brought me to an unknown place. What could I possibly share to leave an impact? I wasn't a bestseller. I wasn't an entertainment mogul. I wasn't a megachurch leader. Who would want to listen to me? With all the questions swirling, I chose to create anyway, to be faithful with a humble seed, to wander in the sacred resistance.

Voices battled against my thoughts as I outlined and rehearsed my keynote. My mind flashed to one of the times when I'd spoken in front of an audience after returning from a mission trip to the Philippines. Members of our team had shared their experience and how Presence showed up in amazing ways. Powerful testimonies. My nerves rattled as I anticipated my turn.

I wish I could say the seas parted and the mountains trembled, but the truth is most of what I shared was in a fog. For some reason, my words shifted toward sharing about a center in the barrios of Cebu where missionaries and midwives delivered newborns—next door to a slaughterhouse. I was on the verge of blacking out, but my mouth kept moving. I was fixated on one aspect of the delivery: a birthing stool. Let's just say my demonstration on how the stool worked dug an even deeper hole.

At one point, I glanced toward the back of the sanctuary where the wife stood and tried to reassure her, "Don't worry, I know how babies are born." The congregation erupted in laughter, which did nothing to boost my dwindling confidence. Sweat seeped down my spine as I awkwardly stepped back from the microphone.

So much for miracles.

Later, I returned to Estes Park, Colorado, to speak again. Past experiences of failing to communicate in front of a live audience streamed through my mind on repeat. My nerves rattled when I was introduced to more seasoned session and keynote speakers. I mustered up enough courage to get through the reception dinner before escaping to my room. Following a restless night, a bone-chilling morning welcomed the inevitable.

After years of creating in obscurity and weeks of preparation to speak, I stepped onto the stage. As the audience waited, my nervousness vanished. I'd never experienced a weight being lifted so easily. For the next forty minutes, words flowed and the message delivered with clarity and conviction. Laughter. Tears. Encouragement. Challenges. Faithfulness in Presence. A walk with Wonder. A touch from Creativity. All rooted in stories from the margins and seasons in the wild.

Fellow creatives applauded as I stepped off the stage. But the reward wasn't in the applause; it was in the calling. My words were not my own. I'd witnessed Presence, in His majesty and wonder, expand my creativity by gifting me the courage to stand strong. He did the rest.

A breakthrough happened that morning, even though no one else realized the battle in my soul. Presence turned a keynote into a rallying cry for creatives. He'd prepared me for this moment, even when I didn't realize it was happening, years before the floodgates opened. He stood with me in the fire—beyond the familiar, beyond the comfortable.

Buried doesn't mean dead.

When we lead and create with curiosity, we witness seeds we've buried in creative ditches sprout above ground. In the margins, we remain curious as we lead with awe and step toward the edge of brave. And we don't go alone: We go with Presence. We don't surrender to our fear. Instead, we encounter courage beyond ourselves. We chase creativity and welcome wonder, free from expectations and the unexpected to create in ways we never imagined.

In the margins, Presence guides us deeper than we ever thought possible. Along winding trails, steep paths, death-defying descents, and endless deserts. Even into places we're not sure we belong. He leads us there anyway. In those places, we learn that the art of the margins moves us to lead with wonder—to walk in expectation of how Presence will use us in new and curious seasons.

We must remain ready for unexpected moments when our posture of wonder is a weapon against apathy. When seasons in the wilderness leave us exhausted, spiritually dry, and with a lack of passion for our craft, wonder is the weapon that will help us fight back.

> Blessed are you who give yourselves over to GOD,
> turn your backs on the world's "sure thing,"
> ignore what the world worships;

The world's a huge stockpile
of GOD-wonders and God-thoughts.
Nothing and no one
compares to you! (Psalm 40:4–5a)

On this great adventure, we have a choice to chase the world or chase the wonder. We weren't created to dig our own graves alone in a creative graveyard. When we chase the wonder, we till the earth, plant seeds, and water the soil as Presence breathes oxygen into our creative souls. We inhale the beauty and mystery of what He is growing beneath the surface of ordinary. And we exhale onto blank pages, refusing to settle for the world, the culture, or anything less than a legacy rooted in the wonder of Presence.

The wonder of Presence is sacred. It's the lens that allows us to see possibility in wilderness seasons, potential in overlooked people, and purpose in our creativity others have given up on. In a world obsessed with certainty, wonder chooses awe. Wonder walks slower. Wonder listens longer. Wonder dreams deeper. Wonder invites us to lead in awe of Presence. If we lead from wonder, we become architects of hope, builders of worlds, and catalysts of change.

Lead the way with wonder. Lead the way in humility. Lead the way in love. Lead beyond our visions, to inspire, to walk, to create with, to bring fresh creativity beyond the confines of a church, an industry, or a culture. Wonder welcomes others into the margins to encounter an epic journey too, one that will find us standing together in the fire.

Wonder allows us to conquer our fears to create in unexpected places and unimaginable ways. It won't always be on a stage. It won't always be on a list or a chart. It won't always be in front of the masses. But it will always be significant in the eyes of Presence. Creating in wonder, our harshest fears push us toward the sacred resistance where holy toughness is forged. Where we are compelled to create beyond labels, beyond walls, beyond the expected.

When we lead with wonder, we ask, "Presence, where are You guiding me now?" A home. An office. A church. A boardroom. A stage. A gallery. An auditorium. An arena. He reminds us that our past is history and our future in this world is not yet known to us. But we have an eternal promise that brings us to our knees beside our creative ditches. There we will learn to surrender the outcome to Presence. In this moment, right now, we can find the courage and bravery to lead with wonder.

18

CALLING BENEATH THE CRAFT

Bright streaks of light flashed across the night sky. As the turbulence intensified, I witnessed the beauty of Presence through the lens of an oval window from my economy seat. First, a vibrant sunset had painted a masterpiece of flaming orange and ocean blue. Now, a glowing full moon brightened the night as thunder and lightning performed on a heavenly stage.

For hours, I unplugged and lost myself in wonder.

Unplugged was what I needed. A moment to reflect on more than the work. In many ways, it was a chance to breathe in the in-between. Sometimes that's what we need most. We don't need another task, another milestone, another ideation, another sermon, another story, another creative endeavor. We just need to be still and surrender to the wonder of Presence. That's not always easy, especially when we're in the grind. We get good at the task, and autopilot is a quick switch. But this was one of those times where Presence had my undivided attention.

One day earlier, I had boarded a rickety boat in Manaus, Brazil, and inhaled a pungent odor of petrol. Minutes from shore, we were lost in a winding river surrounded by an immense jungle. Welcome to the Amazon. One of my favorite novels, *The Testament*, brings readers to the heart of this jungle. It's still at the top of my Grisham list, even though it may not be his best known. He remains an inspiration as a storyteller, and this tale captured my heart. When I finished reading the last page, I thought, *Yes, this is what I'm called to do.*

After an incredible experience hiking through the jungle, which included meeting a local man who showed us his collection of tarantulas, I was on a flight to São Paulo. And the lightning show over the Amazon was my front-row seat to the magnificent power of Presence. I was in one of those seasons fighting against the margins. I was afraid of being written off the page, being left on the editing room floor. I wasn't on a quest to catch an anaconda either. I'd met a few in ministry and entertainment who were just as slippery and deadly. No, I was struggling to understand the difference between identity and calling—the calling beneath the craft.

On this trip, I'd eaten plenty of Brazilian barbecue to help me get to the bottom of the mystery. Can I get an amen? Anyone who knows me knows a love of red meat flows through my veins. I'll try any diet as long as there's rib eye and filet mignon.

A pastor and politician had even closed down a restaurant for a special dinner—a *rodízio*. Over the course of an hour, the waiters brought skewers of meat and sliced one serving after another onto my plate. Not wanting to disrespect or offend, I accepted the challenge and finished off six plates of food. I'd eaten so much that I was sweating and needed a third bottle of Coke to get the rest down. Still, the waiters sliced just one more piece.

You see, one of my friends who traveled with me had played a trick. While everyone else had a small wooden block painted half red and half green near their plate, mine was nowhere to be found. I never even noticed it was or wasn't there in the first place. As the second hour passed, the waiters' eyes grew bigger each time they sliced another stack of meat onto my plate. I'd lost count and kept eating until my friend handed me a colored block and explained that turning the red side up means the waiters can stop serving you. Game over. We all had a good laugh ... and I waddled back to the hotel beyond stuffed.

I couldn't get the waiters to stop. I couldn't get the world to slow down. I couldn't separate identity from calling. Until I chose between red or green.

Without fully realizing it, my identity had become engrained in the work. I'm not sure how it happened or when it happened, but there was no denying: My worth was woven into my creativity expressed for others. It was a unique skill set, yet not always who I was called to be. That may sound strange, but it was the truth, and it left an underlying restlessness. Many of my decisions were made based on others' needs, not necessarily on my calling.

That's when the wooden block flipped red.

On the late-night flight over the Amazon, Presence unplugged the world around me to grab my attention. Remembering the eating frenzy at the rodízio offered a revelation: My creativity needed to be rooted in my calling, not my identity. My craft needed to be an outpouring of my calling, not a way to advance my own purpose through others.

That flipped the wooden block green.

> For we are God's handiwork, created in Christ Jesus to do good works, which God prepared in advance for us to do. (Eph. 2:10 NIV)

Presence often hides calling in the ordinary, even when identity is extraordinary. He reveals truth in the margins beyond the walls of ambition. Calling doesn't compete with craft; it breathes beneath creativity. We're not just creating ... we're being made in His image. We're not what we create; we're who we're becoming. Calling isn't found beyond the work. It's formed within it.

In the quiet rhythm of the work, Presence shapes us with a solid foundation, a steady platform to create. It's in those seasons of seeking more of Him and less of us that faithfulness becomes the brush of humility that paints every true calling. We become more aware of a passion to uncover our calling beneath the craft. We aren't the sum of our ideas. We aren't the number of followers, likes, finished projects, or client rosters. We aren't even our most creative work. Creativity is a gift, but it's not our identity. Creativity is our calling. Our craft isn't just what we create—it's how Presence made and shapes us.

Too many of us have mistaken talent for calling. We've built our worth on applause and our identity on output. We work harder, longer, and faster, believing this will give us satisfaction. But when the well runs dry—when the seeds stop growing, the audience stops clapping, the ideas stop flowing, the ministry stops reaching, and the business plateaus—who are we then?

If we struggle to answer this question, then we are battling between surrendering our identity and serving in our calling. When we look in the mirror, who stares back at us? All of the sacrifice and work will leave us feeling like something is missing. Talent will take us only so far, but it will always leave us searching for more. Talent will derail calling if we allow it. The more talented we are, the more we risk drifting further away from who Presence called us to become.

We walk into a room or onto a stage and rely on our creativity and skills instead of humbly surrendering our calling to Presence. No one may ever know it's happening. Our talent camouflages an identity where we've stopped rooting ourselves in humility and faithfulness. Instead, we've allowed ourselves to be lured away from where our creativity is forged.

In the margins, we must search for a calling beyond the talent.

And we must dig deep for our calling beneath the craft.

Simon was a fisherman called by Jesus to be one of the twelve disciples. He was known for his boldness and even brashness at times. Jesus even renamed him Peter—*Cephas*, which means "rock" in Aramaic[5]:

> My Father in heaven, God himself, let you in on this secret of who I really am. And now I'm going to tell you who you are, *really* are. You are Peter, a rock. This is the rock on which I will put together my church, a church so expansive with energy that not even the gates of hell will be able to keep it out. (Matt. 16:17b–18, italics in original)

Peter's identity was in catching fish; Presence was teaching him to catch souls. The nets weren't the calling—they were the training. In the routine of casting nets, Jesus called him to cast faith. He went from red to green at a thunderous pace.

From fisherman to Jesus' inner circle, a bystander to a witness of miracles. Peter even walked on water ... until doubt crept in, and he started sinking. He also denied Jesus three times before His crucifixion—a trifecta of holy failure that can happen to any of us. But Jesus restored him after the resurrection. And after the ascension, Peter became a cornerstone in the early Church. He preached with conviction, faced persecution, and died a martyr in the faith.

Before the masterpiece, there's the margin. A fisherman who became a disciple of Jesus. A disciple who became a friend of the Son of Presence. A friend who became a denier of the Messiah. A denier restored who became the rock of the church. There's hope for all of us.

I'd love to walk in the wild with Peter. So much in common, so much to learn. We'd enjoy a Brazilian barbecue and hide the wooden block for a while. He understood the calling beneath the craft. He unplugged from being a fisherman to encounter true purpose. He stepped away from luring fish to capture hearts. From the shotgun seat of the greatest story ever told, his purpose shifted from surviving to surrender, from striving to serving. When he witnessed the miraculous power of Presence as calling, everything changed. Eternity changed.

On this dirt road in the wild, we discover the path of Presence. We unplug from our identity and plug into the gift of creativity in our calling. We don't create to prove something. We don't create to be someone. We create because we are entrusted with a gift rooted in forgiveness, grace, love, and eternity. We create because there is a story that must be told. We begin to lead with purpose, not pressure. With conviction, not comparison. And our creative fire in calling was never meant to burn alone—it's meant to light the way for others.

In the calling beneath the craft, Presence is not asking for perfection; He's inviting participation. We don't fight the margins; we welcome them. We don't strive for identity; we surrender to calling—every time. We don't clean ourselves up to walk with Presence; we walk with Presence to clean ourselves up.

We leave our identity at the threshold when we step into the edge of brave in our calling. That is the art of the margins. That is the magnificent power of thunder and lightning in the night sky.

19

REVELATION OF THE MARGINS

Amidst the silence of obscurity, Presence forges voices that don't echo culture—they disrupt it. In the wild wastelands of creative destiny, prophets are shaped, revolutions are born, and truth is carried with fire in its bones. Margins aren't a detour or a dead end—they're on the edge of divine strategy that burns away the illusion of performance and leaves only raw, real, and eternal purpose. No longer identity but forever calling. When we create from the margins, we're not waiting to be found—we're already standing on holy ground.

Jesus is the genesis and revelation of the margins. He isn't a prophet who wandered in the wilderness; He is the beginning and the end. He is the spark to a revolution rooted in truth, and His creativity changes everything. Born in the margins, He didn't enter this world in a palace but in a stable. His first cradle was a feeding trough. His first visitors were shepherds, not kings. From his first breath, Jesus identified with those who had no voice: outsiders, forgotten, those whom society overlooked.

> Think of yourselves the way Christ Jesus thought of himself. He had equal status with God but didn't think so much of himself that he had to cling to the advantages of that status no matter what. Not at all. When the time came, he set aside the privileges of deity and took on the status of a slave, became *human*! Having become human, he stayed human. It was an incredibly humbling process. He didn't claim special privileges. Instead, he lived a selfless, obedient life and then died a selfless, obedient death—and the worst kind of death at that—a crucifixion. (Phil. 2:7–8, italics in original)

When I think about this deeply, chills shoot through my soul. Miraculous. Epic. Truth. Am I willing to live in this same way as a wanderer and creative?

Jesus defined the edge of brave. To think: The Savior of the world didn't come through the halls of power but through a borrowed manger—a declaration the margins are where Presence begins His greatest work.

We are reminded that sacred work often starts in overlooked places.

Jesus awakened His movement not among the elite or influential, but among fishermen, tax collectors, women, and lepers. He sought out those whom society rejected—the poor, the sick, the sinner, the Samaritan. He preached in the temples, but He rejected being controlled by the Pharisees. His table became the center of a revolution: He broke bread with the broken. He gave dignity to the dismissed. He restored the outcasts to community.

> For the Son of Man came to find and restore the lost. (Luke 19:10)

In the overlooked places where others avoided sinners, He welcomed sons and daughters. Where others labeled waste, He named worth. He revealed the Kingdom of Presence rising from the edges, not the center, of the page. He spoke not merely about Presence but as Presence. Like the prophets of old, Jesus confronted hypocrisy, called people to repentance, and announced the coming of a Kingdom ruled by Presence. But unlike any prophet before, He embodied the message He proclaimed and welcomed those in the margins to walk alongside.

> God's Spirit is on me;
> he's chosen me to preach the Message of good news to the poor,
> sent me to announce pardon to prisoners and
> recovery of sight to the blind,
> to set the burdened and the battered free,
> to announce, "This is God's time to shine!" (Luke 4:18–19)

Jesus made history. He was the very reason history existed. He was the fulfillment of prophecy. He was the One sent to save the world. He was Revelation to a revolution whose words pierced systems, not just hearts—speaking truth to power, to religion, and empire alike. In his arsenal of spiritual weapons were creativity, compassion, and love. He was a storyteller through culture-shifting parables that enraged the religious elite. He walked with those seen as less than, and yet He embraced them right where they were, calling them to Himself.

He proclaimed a Kingdom that upside-downed the world. He launched the most profound revolution in history—not through violence, but through love. He overturned tables, yes, but also upended the entire definition of what power means in religion and culture. The weak were blessed, the proud were brought low, and the first became last.

> "My kingdom," said Jesus, "doesn't consist of what you see around you. If it did, my followers would fight so that I wouldn't be handed over to the Jews. But I'm not that kind of king, not the world's kind of king." (John 18:36)

His revolution was spiritual, social, and eternal—redefining freedom, justice, and victory. In the margins, the stones cry out for this same revolution. We've seen how religion and culture mirror one another in many ways. But in the Kingdom of Presence, in the wild of the margins, in Revelation's call to a revolution, all of this is stripped away in an upside-down world.

Maybe it's time we flipped a few tables in our churches, ministries, and businesses. Maybe it's time preferred parking was reserved for those in need. Maybe it's time we dug a deeper creative ditch to find greater purpose. Maybe it's time our calling shook the culture. Maybe it's time we served others rather than being served because of our creativity.

When the religious and political systems sought to silence Jesus, truth was revealed in the margins. He didn't fight for the throne: He carried a cross.

Crucified outside the city walls—literally on the margins—He showed that redemption and revolution begin where rejection reigns. The cross, a symbol of defeat, became the ultimate revelation of love and victory.

> He was crucified outside the city gates—*that* is where he poured out the sacrificial blood that was brought to God's altar to cleanse his people. (Heb. 13:12, italics in original)

The truth of Presence's power was not revealed in dominance but in surrender. Not in wealth but in sacrifice. Not in fame but in faithfulness. Jesus is the Truth—the Revelation of Presence Himself.

> Jesus said, "I am the Road, also the Truth, also the Life. No one gets to the Father apart from me. If you really knew me, you would know my Father as well. From now on, you do know him. You've even seen him!" (John 14:6–7)

He revealed that truth isn't just a concept—it's a person. He is the Revelation of the heart of Presence, the mirror of divine love, and the light that exposes darkness. He is Creativity. In Him, truth and revelation are one. In Him, every falsehood falls away. And in Him, the revolution of grace and love begins. From the margins, He spoke truth to the center and built a Kingdom outward. He revealed the margins as the holy ground between heaven and earth.

After the resurrection, the revolution continued through people who lived in the margins: persecuted believers, exiled disciples, the nameless who carried the message forward throughout the centuries. The gospel spread from the streets, not the Senate; from prisons, not the palaces; from homes, not hierarchy. That's where truth takes root—in the overlooked, underestimated places where Presence writes His greatest stories.

To follow Jesus today means to believe He is still moving. He's found in the shelters and the schools, in the single mother's resilience and the refugee's prayer. He's with the artist who paints hope on cracked walls and the songwriter chasing every lyric, the entrepreneur who sacrifices for a dream and the teacher who refuses to give up on her students, the preacher who weighs every word and the leader who chooses integrity over identity or influence.

Jesus in the margins reminds us that transformation rarely starts in the headlines—it begins in the hidden places. The Kingdom of Presence doesn't flow from the top down, but from the margins. And that's where creativity, compassion, and calling take root: wherever love chooses to show up in the shadows of the wilderness.

The margins are the new mainstream, and we are the Truth-tellers.

We are the revolutionaries of Revelation, and our weapon is creativity.

In the digital age, the gatekeepers have fallen. Once, access to influence ran through traditional institutions. Today, anyone with a phone can share a message to reach the world. That's profoundly biblical. Jesus didn't build a platform through empire channels, and my guess is He wouldn't be consumed with likes, follows, or shares on Instagram, TikTok, or X. Those are creative tools not worthy of our worship. Revelation built a movement through relationship, story, and Presence. We are called to do the same.

Likewise, digital platforms have become the modern margins—places where new voices emerge, where truth, creativity, and justice move without institutional permission. In some countries, this freedom is being challenged right now. But the digital revolution has, in many ways, democratized what Revelation modeled: Presence working through ordinary people in unexpected places.

Jesus' ministry was countercultural. He told parables that disrupted systems and flipped assumptions. In the same way, creativity in culture today that originates in the margins, outside the algorithms of conformity and commercialism, still has the power to subvert the noise of digital sameness. There has never been a more powerful moment for creatives than this day.

We must choose the margins, to wander in the wild, to stand on the edge of brave. We must be willing to flip a few tables, splatter a few canvases, and create with resilient courage. We must surrender ourselves fully and walk in the wilderness alongside Revelation and Presence.

The future of creativity will belong not to those who shout the loudest, not to those who are sheep to culture, but to those who listen deepest—who create work born out of empathy, authenticity, and purpose. The margins remind us that success isn't viral reach; it's eternal impact. But the danger of the digital age is disconnection … where our presence becomes pixels and relationships become reaction.

Jesus shows us a different way: creativity rooted in embodiment. In the margins, we must dig deeper to rediscover creativity that connects people back to real stories and authentic experiences. Yes, our creativity can provide an escape and entertainment, but what happens when the story ends? What will we leave with readers, listeners, viewers? The same is true for entrepreneurs, business leaders, and even our churches. After the product is purchased, the client is served, and the sermon is preached, what will we leave to move others toward Presence?

Creators inspired by the margins understand this intuitively. For many, this is the very reason we create in the first place. We aren't building brands; we're building bridges. Our creativity restores human dignity, cultivates belonging, and turns screens into sacred spaces for encounter. Innovation in the margins comes from the edges, not the center. The early church grew from small gatherings, not cathedrals. The Renaissance was birthed in workshops, not royal courts. Today, the most transformative creativity is emerging from overlooked creators—those outside traditional systems of power or privilege.

Jesus in the margins reminds us the next revolution in creativity won't be technological … it will be spiritual. It will come from those who create with conviction, compassion, and courage, not just code. If the first digital revolution democratized creativity, the next will spiritualize it. The future belongs to creatives who merge faith and innovation, who see technology not as a tool for fame but as a canvas for redemption.

The margins aren't where Presence hides; they're where He reveals what's to come. And in a world of artificial intelligence and digital excess, the most human, sacred, and Spirit-filled creativity will shine brightest. You see, Jesus entered the margins to redeem humanity. We enter the margins in search of His heart, and He walks with us in the wild as Revelation. Our mission and call are united: Bring light to hidden places, hope to lost wanderers, and prove the art of the margins still changes everything.

I'm more convinced of this today than ever before. I've got the battle scars to prove it. From building an indie label in a church to launching a creative house to producing and directing to releasing stories as an indie and traditionally published author, I'm on the front lines without boundaries. Presence has brought me through the fire, and He'll do the same for you.

The margins aren't where you're left behind—they're where you're forged. You have a choice to pursue the calling of Jesus or create in the status quo. Surrender means fighting with resilience and determination on this side. Creativity promises to walk with you in the margins to reach the lost. You're not bound by tradition; you're set free as a follower of Revelation as you raise your weapon of creativity to fight in a revolution for souls.

20

MADE TO BE ORIGINAL

A widow. A foreigner. A woman without status.

Ruth's world was defined by scarcity and sorrow. Her husband was gone, her home was gone, and the future she imagined had vanished. In that broken space, in the margins, her calling began to take shape. When Naomi, her mother-in-law, urged her to return to her own people, Ruth made a choice that defied logic and expectation. Her words echo through history:

> Where you go, I go; and where you live, I'll live. Your people are my people, your God is my god; where you die, I'll die, and that's where I'll be buried, so help me GOD—not even death itself is going to come between us! (Ruth 1:16b–17)

Ruth's decision to stay with Naomi led her to Bethlehem—where she was unseen, unknown, scraping in the fields for leftover grain. Yet that field became her canvas. She made a declaration of covenant loyalty, not ambition. Her faith was expressed through action, not platform. Her creativity was born from surrender, not status. Her quiet work in the margins caught the attention of Boaz, a man of standing, who recognized in her something rare: steadfastness, integrity, and courage.

Hit the pause button for a moment.

Loyalty. Faith in action. Surrender. Quiet work.

Steadfastness. Integrity. Courage.

Is this forging of creativity and leadership always forefront? We might say it is true, and we might proclaim it in front of the masses, but when we step deeper into the margins and wander for a while, do we truly believe the same? Ambition. Platform. Status. Oftentimes those rise to the top, camouflaged as cultural relevance and religious influence.

But the margins guide us down the same path as Ruth.

And what unfolds next reveals divine artistry.

Presence weaved the story of Ruth—a marginalized widow from Moab—into the lineage of King David and, ultimately, into the genealogy of Jesus. What the world overlooked, Presence redeemed. What others called small, Presence called sacred. What began in the margins became central to His redemptive story. Ruth embodied the message at the heart of the margins. Sacred work began in obscurity, not in a place of punishment but in a place of preparation. The masterpieces of Presence are often painted with colors of humility, faith, and persistence ... on the canvas of ordinary life.

Ruth reminds us creativity, calling, and redemption often take root where the world sees nothing of value. Her legacy is proof that faithfulness in the margins leads to fruitfulness in our creativity. She wasn't trying to stand out; she was simply being faithful. Her originality came from obedience, not ambition. When she chose to follow Naomi, she stepped into an unknown season in the wilderness that didn't belong to anyone else.

Why? She was created to be original.

Ruth entered a foreign land as one of the poor and engaged in grueling manual labor. She embraced a calling outside the center of power. Yet it was there, in the margins, where her faithfulness became a story of redemption woven into the lineage of Revelation.

True originality begins when we stop chasing what's popular and start walking in the wild on the path Presence sets before us. Creativity that impacts culture isn't a reboot—it's an original calling. And the margins are often where the most original work is born: outside the spotlight, where faith and grit collide. Originality doesn't require status; it requires courageous surrender. Ruth's story transformed ordinary acts—gleaning in fields, honoring relationships, trusting Presence—into the framework of divine creativity. Her originality was quiet but revolutionary.

The art of the margins reminds us that originality isn't about novelty; it's about bringing divine purpose into ordinary places. The most transformative ideas often come from unseen faithfulness. Our lives become a pattern of redemptive creativity: Presence uses our story to bridge cultures, rewrite legacies, and bring forth renewed life. We are made to be original, to allow Presence to write His creativity through us, to bridge what's broken and birth redemption through our unique creative expression.

We weren't created to blend in; we were crafted to break through. In a world that celebrates the copy-and-paste culture of trends and algorithms, the rarest expression is when we offer our true voice. The most unforgettable work—the kind that stirs hearts, touches souls, and shifts culture—doesn't come from formulas. It comes from fire. From soul. From the deep reservoir of who we are and what we've walked through.

Like Ruth, we are made to be original too.

For those of us who are wanderers of Revelation, we must fight the temptation to chase the world, the trending artistic expressions, and the outward celebrity. Presence is calling us back to the wild to unearth raw, honest creativity ... not curated for clicks or streams but grown from conviction. When we create from those creative ditches, our work won't just resonate—it will reverberate to heaven.

One of my all-time favorite films is *Man on Fire*. In my opinion, it's one of Denzel Washington's very best, and Dakota Fanning was equally as brilliant. Denzel in the role of John Creasy is not just another performance—it is a master class in purpose-driven creativity. Creasy, a former assassin numbed by failure and guilt, becomes the unlikely guardian of a girl in Mexico City.

What begins as a story of protection unfolds into one of redemption. Beneath the action and intensity lies a profound transformation: a man rediscovering his reason to live through the act of sacrifice, and a girl whose faith and belief kept her alive when darkness swarmed.

In an era where performances often lead to spectacle, Denzel stood out through restraint. His power was found in presence. Each line, pause, and decision felt grounded, deliberate, alive. He didn't perform the part; he *inhabited* it. His originality wasn't about being different; it was about being true. He anchored his craft in integrity, allowing the work to speak for itself.

In *Man on Fire*, he captures what many creatives and leaders forget: Originality is not about performance, it's about conviction. And sometimes we have to be willing to sacrifice and fight to keep that conviction alive. The most compelling stories emerge when we stop chasing attention and start creating in truth. Denzel's artistry reminds us creativity becomes powerful not when it's loud but when it's honest.

Every artist faces the temptation to imitate, but originality is born when we create from conviction, not comparison. When we stop trying to fit into culture and instead allow our work to reflect the holy fire inside of us. True originality carries a quiet confidence. Originality is not reactive to culture—it's rooted in calling.

Authenticity is the birthplace of originality. Denzel's performance resonates because it's grounded in truth, not trend. Ease dulls creativity; struggle refines it. Growth comes from the tension and resistance. Great work doesn't demand attention; it commands presence through integrity and focus. Purpose outlasts the applause. When we create for a greater purpose than recognition, our impact in the revolution endures long after the battles fade.

We stop striving to be seen and begin surrendering to the guidance of Presence as our work becomes sacred. Originality isn't the product of ambition—it's the fruit of obedience. It's found in unseen places in the wild where we choose faithfulness over fame and calling over copying, because we are wonderfully and uniquely made.

> Oh yes, you shaped me first inside, then out;
>   you formed me in my mother's womb.
> I thank you, High God—you're breathtaking!
>   Body and soul, I am marvelously made!
>   I worship in adoration—what a creation!

> You know me inside and out,
> you know every bone in my body;
> you know exactly how I was made, bit by bit,
> how I was sculpted from nothing into something.
> Like an open book, you watched me grow from conception to birth;
> all the stages of my life were spread out before you,
> the days of my life all prepared
> before I'd even lived one day. (Psalm 139:13–16)

In the margins, much like Ruth gleaning in the fields and Denzel embodying conviction in front of the lens, obedience isn't about outcome. It's about offering our best with open hands, trusting Presence to use our surrendered creativity. Originality isn't only about inventing something new; it's about revealing something true. Presence isn't asking us to build or create something impressive: He is asking us to be faithful with what He's already placed in us. That's where originality comes alive—in the tension between fear, failure, and faith—where obedience becomes a pillar of fire that ignites creativity.

I've spent seasons digging creative ditches hoping to reach the right audience or gain approval, and all along, Presence has reminded me to be original. I've battled the urge to strive for platforms instead of creating from surrender. To stop trying to make a name and remain rooted in carrying His name. I haven't always followed the path. But I can say, from silence to surrender, originality without alignment leads to exhaustion. And that truth, as ancient as it is relevant, is found in one of Scripture's earliest creative cautionary tales: the Tower of Babel.

The story of the Tower of Babel is one of the earliest warnings against creative drifts from Presence. People came together with a bold vision—to build a tower to reach the heavens, to make a name for themselves. Unity.

Ambition. Skill. But they had lost alignment. Their creativity was no longer rooted beneath the soil in obedience; it was drowned in pride.

Presence didn't condemn their ability to build—He questioned their motive for building. What they designed to elevate themselves ended up dividing them. Their language fractured, their purpose scattered, and the work that began in confidence ended in confusion.

Babel teaches us the originality of creation is not elevation; it's alignment. When we use our gifts to make our name known instead of the name of Presence, we lose the language that unites heaven and earth. When we create from surrender, our work expresses worship to the One who is greater than all others.

We still live in a world of towers. Only now, they're built from influence, followers, and metrics. Our bricks are digital; our mortar is ambition. But the same questions resonate: Why are we building? Why are we creating? Who are we serving?

Presence isn't impressed by our platforms—He's drawn to our posture. He's not asking us to climb higher but to dig deeper, to build meaning instead of monuments. Creativity detached from obedience leads to confusion, but creativity rooted in surrender leads to communion.

In the margins, our art is simple and sacred. We don't create to be seen; we create to serve. We don't strive to make our name great; we trust Presence to make our work eternal. We don't stack stones to build towers; we dig creative ditches and build altars on the rock.

Babel leaves us standing in the dust of our own blueprints, asking what kind of wanderers we'll be in the wild on an epic adventure toward revolution. It's a mirror for every creative, entrepreneur, and leader who's ever felt the desire to prove instead of the call to serve. I've chased belonging, recognition, and results, but in the end, Presence reminds me how His greatest work isn't built on platforms ... it's forged in the margins.

An invitation to the margins is for all of us: to tear down our towers, pick up our shovels, dig creative ditches, and surrender the outcome with humility and holy intent. That's where originality is born—in the quiet spaces where Presence whispers our foundation and creativity becomes an outpouring of our worship to Him.

We were made to be original. Authentic. We weren't made to imitate. We were made to initiate. Culture needs what only we can create. It's not about building towers to showcase our skills. It's not even about breaking rules. It's about running free.

Originality isn't confined to the arts: It's the language of calling in motion. It's not just for authors, filmmakers, or musicians. It's for entrepreneurs building businesses to serve rather than exploit. It's for leaders who choose integrity over identity or influence. It's for faith leaders who preach truth when silence would be safer. It's for the quiet innovators who see what could be and refuse to accept the status quo.

Every creative act—whether we're shaping a brand, creating art, leading a team, designing a product, or crafting a sermon—begins with one question: Will I make what's been done or ignite what's been given?

In the art of the margins, we learn the call of a creative is to trust the design of Presence in us. To create, lead, and live from the convictions He's placed deep within our souls. To resist the pressure to conform, to silence the noise long enough to hear His whisper, and to follow Him into the unknown.

When we listen and obey, our work becomes more than output—it becomes an offering. We don't need to be louder ... we need to be truer. The world doesn't need more noise; it needs more courage. Be original. Be faithful. Be who Presence called you to be—no more, no less. Because the greatest act of creativity is not found in imitation. It's unearthed when the holy fire that Presence places within us finally becomes a pillar of radiant light in the wild.

21

RETURN TO AWE

Ten years in the making.

A whisper of a story that wouldn't let go. A boy caught between worlds, standing at the threshold of light and darkness. I'd listened to Jack's voice in my imagination for years and was haunted by the spark of *Beacon Hill* through the wilderness seasons. Creativity's whisper wouldn't let go. Scenes were left as notes. Dialogue was an ongoing internal conversation. Fragments of a world with no home on the page. For years, the idea lived quietly in the margins, being watered from time to time.

Awe-inspired stories don't fade: They wait before they're awakened.

Moses's ordinary day in the wilderness was interrupted by a moment of wonder—a bush that burned but was not consumed. This divine encounter reignited purpose within a man who had fled from destiny. Awe restored his courage and creativity to lead a nation. "God said, 'Don't come any closer. Remove your sandals from your feet. You're standing on holy ground'" (Ex. 3:5).

Awe awakened calling on holy ground.

After the success of *The Auctioneer*, my plan was to write the second book in the series. But that wasn't the holy ground Presence prepared in the wild. During a year in post-production on over fifty episodes of television, the creative momentum was rooted in creating for others. And then I was approached to pitch *Beacon Hill* again.

I wasn't seeking an opportunity, but the bush was already burning. Years in the margins, and I was still learning the art of surrender. I wasn't always successful, but I was always willing. I was reminded to create without an attachment to outcome, but with wonder. In the quietness of the wild, prayers were whispered rooted in trust and obedience and were their own reward.

Wonder is the birthplace of creativity.

> God looked over everything he had made;
> it was so good, so very good!

It was evening, it was morning—
Day Six. (Gen. 1:31)

The original story of creation is the ultimate expression of divine imagination. Presence spoke light, color, form, and life into existence, revealing how creativity begins with wonder. Humanity, made in His image, carries the same spark of wonder that inspired creation. We are created to be original: no expectation, just availability to be used in His calling for our lives. We are His creation designed to create beyond Day Six.

After years of silence in the wilderness for *Beacon Hill*, the story that had lived in my heart and soul for over a decade still breathed. In the margins, Presence moved at the pace of my obedience before unfolding an opportunity. A publishing deal came together nearly as fast as creation itself. The excitement was real ... but so was the weight of the journey ahead. Now this story wasn't a dream: It was a deadline.

> The whole earth is filled with awe at your wonders; where morning dawns, where evening fades, you call forth songs of joy. (Ps. 65:8 NIV)

The joy of the first morning as I sat down to *officially* write *Hunt for Eden's Star*, the first book in the *Beacon Hill* series, is engrained in my soul. A quiet hotel room and a blank page glowing in the half-light of dawn. Ten years of notes, scenes, and prayers led up to this moment. The cursor blinked, steady and expectant. This was the unknown. This was the beginning. And for a long moment, I stared at the screen in awe of Presence—grateful, steady, and expectant.

Awe transforms and commissions.

We've seen this when Isaiah beheld the glory of the Lord—amidst seraphim, smoke, and holiness—and his creative voice was renewed. Out of awe came purification and purpose, birthing one of the most poetic prophetic books in Scripture. "Holy, Holy, Holy is GOD-of-the-Angel-Armies. His bright glory fills the whole earth .... 'Whom shall I send? Who will go for us?' I spoke up, 'I'll go. Send me!'" (Isa. 6:3b, 8b)

Barefoot that morning in the hotel room, I sensed the stillness of answered prayers and being commissioned to write an epic tale not only to entertain but to bring the message of Presence. *I'll go. Send me!* Unseen obedience, not always perfect, came before the breakthrough. Now in its place was the weight of stepping beyond the edge of brave toward wonder.

Oftentimes we forget how to be amazed between our creative endeavors. We trade mystery for mastery. Beauty for busyness. Bare feet for worn boots. But awe is not optional for the creative—it's our oxygen. When a dream finally becomes real, awe and fear arrive in unison. Suddenly, we're not just imagining what could be: We're responsible for what is and will be.

In the margins, a posture of awe and wonder slows the spin of the world just long enough for the soul to breathe. Our gaze is lifted from the grind toward grandeur, reminding us that we don't create to impress—we create to *express* what we've seen, what we've felt, what's lit us up from the inside, and what's inspired us beyond culture.

Once again, we're invited to return to the wonder that started it all—astonished in creation by Presence, amazed to be creating through our relationship with Revelation. If we're entrusted with creativity, then we must pray in obedience and create faithfully between those moments of awe. That's what will root us when the harvest breaks through.

To keep the story alive, I sought places of sanctuary to create: hidden spaces where silence spoke louder than the sounds of production, phone calls, emails, texts, meetings, and the routine of ordinary life.

There was a small cottage veiled in the mists of Northern California's wine country, where dawn unfolded in soft grays and the stillness carried its own kind of melody. It felt otherworldly, like stepping through a doorway into an imaginary world. In the quiet, I heard the story breathe.

There was a beach house in Malibu, perched high above the Pacific, where the waves kept time with the rhythm of creation, rushing in with fierce momentum, then pulling back to reveal what had been buried beneath. The sea became my metronome, reminding me how creativity, like the tide, moves in seasons.

And there were the nights in my office when the only light came from the glow of the screen, the hum of the world outside fading into nothing. Those were the hours when the work asked for everything—and returned a calling for an eternal purpose.

As the story, characters, and worlds shifted from black and white to color, these places were sanctuaries, sacred thresholds where the noise of life gave way to the whisper of wonder. Each space was a chapter in its own pilgrimage in the wild. Each reminded me that awe is not a fleeting spark—it's a way of seeing, a way of being on holy ground. Maybe that's why I still write barefoot.

Wonder reawakened joy and purpose.

I think of the shepherds on a hillside who were suddenly surrounded by heaven's glory announcing the birth of Jesus. "The shepherds returned and let loose, glorifying and praising God for everything they had heard and seen. It turned out exactly the way they'd been told!" (Luke 2:20). Their encounter filled them with awe, and awe turned into action. They became the first messengers of the Messiah's arrival.

Awe inspires us to create from Revelation instead of validation. We become the messengers through our creativity. In writing *Hunt for Eden's Star*, I carried this mantra with me from day one. In the years leading up to *Beacon Hill*, I'd dug creative ditches and watered seeds through writing, producing, directing, and creating when no one was watching. Alongside other producers, show concepts and projects were pitched, but those were not always aligned with my calling. In those years of unseen obedience, Presence prepared me and taught me how the hidden work is holy work. That obscurity wasn't punishment; it was preparation for moments like this.

Before we see fruit, we must first dig ditches in the wild.

Those seeds grow beneath the soil and sprout above ground into a harvest.

And after wandering amidst the harvest, we emerge renewed with purpose.

When *Beacon Hill* finally came to life, I realized the waiting is never wasted. Every unseen effort strengthened the creative muscles needed for this epic series. As *Hunt for Eden's Star* unfolded, I realized how much of the margins were written into it. A search beyond identity. A struggle to believe when faith felt fragile. A tension between worlds—one visible, one unseen. My creative soul became more alive when my craft mirrored its wounds. Writing the beginning of *Hunt for Eden's Star* became an act of healing, a rediscovery of hope through story.

Yes, there were moments when doubt returned, when the words stalled and fear whispered that maybe I wasn't the one to write this epic supernatural saga between this world and other realms. Each time, I returned to the margins to root myself in the truth—faith isn't the absence of uncertainty ... it's the courage to create in the midst of it.

All I knew to do was to keep writing. Through the quiet. Through the questions. Through the distractions. Through the realization I wasn't just telling a story—I was living one. The margins taught me that what felt small today might become sacred tomorrow.

When I finally wrote the last line of *Hunt for Eden's Star*, I leaned back in my chair and exhaled. It wasn't relief: It was reverence. The kind of awe that silences you. The kind that makes you remember who gave you the story in the first place. Presence breathed through the work, beyond whatever might happen when the series released to the world. It had taken years for *Beacon Hill* to find its harvest. But in that moment, I knew the waiting had been part of the story all along. And it was only the first book in the series.

I didn't just write *Beacon Hill*; I was shaped through it in the margins. Creativity offered me a glimpse of the future. And there were both fear and awe in my calling.

In the book of Revelation, we find John on Patmos exiled and alone. He encountered the risen Christ in radiant glory. Out of this holy wonder came the most visionary work of Scripture. Awe became the lens of divine creativity and eternal hope.

> Don't fear: I am First, I am Last, I'm Alive. I died, but I came to life, and my life is now forever. See these keys in my hand? They open and lock Death's doors, they open and lock Hell's gates. Now write down everything you see: things that are, things about to be. (Rev. 1:17b–19)

There was a thread woven from this passage to the story that I was writing. I took the words, "Write down everything you see: things that are, things about to be," and rooted them into the *Beacon Hill* series. An act of worship ran wild as Revelation flowed through my craft.

Even now, whenever I sit down to write, I return to this same truth: Creativity is worship. Obedience is the real breakthrough. Awe and wonder are the sacred beginnings of every story worth telling.

Our calling begins long before the first ditch is dug. It starts in the unseen—an idea, a vision, a whisper that refuses to let go. Ten years in the making wasn't about time: It was about transformation. About learning to trust the silence, to worship through the waiting, and to see awe not as a fleeting spark but as a way of recognizing a holy fire beyond this world.

Whether we're leading a team, building a company, raising a family, designing a product, expressing our gifts, or even writing a story, creativity and calling share the same pulse. Both demand faith in the unseen, courage in uncertainty, and a willingness to say yes when the outcome is still unknown.

Creation didn't end on Day Six—it continues through us. Every act of leadership, innovation, or imagination becomes an anchor of divine creativity, a reminder we were made to bring light into dark places. Awe still calls from the wild ... from the blank page and the boardroom, the studio and the classroom, the workshop and the wilderness. It invites us to take off our shoes in reverence and step closer to the flame—to lead, build, and create from holy ground. Because every margin is sacred space, a meeting place between Presence and the created, when the ordinary becomes extraordinary.

Presence spoke galaxies into being and still breathes through our ideas, our leadership, and our art today. Every word, decision, and design becomes a quiet yes to His invitation: Write down everything you see. Lead with what you've been shown. Build what you've been entrusted to create. When we return to awe, we return to the margins—where purpose is refined, calling is clarified, and vision is reborn. And that's where every story worth living begins.

22

SACRED DETOURS

Two disheartened disciples walked away from Jerusalem, their hopes for redemption buried in the tomb. The road to Emmaus was a detour born from disappointment, a path of retreat rather than purpose. But it was on this very road where Jesus—Revelation—appeared, unrecognized, joining them in their confusion. "He asked, 'What's this you're discussing so intently as you walk along?'" (Luke 24:17a).

Speaking with the despair of one whose world has collapsed, Cleopas, one of the two, recounted what had happened to Jesus the Nazarene. They were confused by news the body was gone from the tomb and of angels who said he was alive.

Jesus didn't correct them immediately or demand belief. Instead, He walked with them. He listened. He explained. And only when they made space for Him—inviting Him to stay and eat—did He open their eyes to awe and wonder.

> Didn't we feel on fire as he conversed with us on the road, as he opened up the Scriptures for us? (Luke 24:32)

The sacred often hides in the slow steps of detours. Revelation comes not when we run ahead but when we walk beside Him in our questions. Breaking bread together around the bonfire becomes the moment of recognition. The detour becomes divine direction. In moments when we sense the path leading us away from purpose, the margins guide us back to Presence. We learn not to rush past the mystery but to make space for Presence and Revelation around the bonfire.

As I worked with the publisher on *Beacon Hill*, there was a holy tension: learning to balance on the high wire of control, to listen openly, to see my words through another's perspective, and to stand my ground in the wild. It wasn't just a process to refine the story; it was a season of refining me. Refinement came slowly, in conversations, rounds of edits, unexpected insight, roadblocks, and unforeseen challenges.

The tension is a tug between good and bad, but it's never a negative when positive creativity shines brighter. Each moment of tension becomes an invitation to rediscover the heart of the story and the calling placed on us. But the road will bend. Plans will change. Visions will evolve. What we think is the destination will shift. But detours aren't delays in our calling; they're the doorway to deeper creativity. We won't be prepared for all the twists and turns, but the good news is we won't be alone along the journey either.

Revelation may reroute our steps, not to limit our impact but to multiply it. Oftentimes the pivot isn't about us. It's about making room for others. When we build with others, we unlock a sacred space. Like the disciples on the road to Emmaus, we learn from the art of the margins that refinement happens around the bonfire—not in the moment of triumph, but in shared community and collaboration rooted in humility. But also like the disciples, we will walk through stretches of our journey surrounded by the excitement of this same collaboration and community, while also fighting unexpected moments that leave us disoriented.

Throughout the editorial process for *Hunt for Eden's Star*, the collaboration with the publisher was inspiring, motivating, and encouraging. One of my best editorial experiences. At the same time, my creative team worked diligently. We knew how to dig ditches, so we pushed to release cinematic trailers for the series and even a documentary inviting everyone behind the scenes of writing the first novel. Nearly two million views amplified our audience.

We rolled up our sleeves and reached out to Barnes & Noble stores across the nation, securing hundreds of locations willing to put *Beacon Hill* on their shelves. For the entire series, we booked over thirty dates with Barnes & Noble on the book tour while balancing a full production slate within our creative house. One of my greatest joys in the process was watching the publisher's acquisitions, editorial, and design teams working in tandem while my creative team pushed beyond the page.

With every line edit, every trailer, every soundtrack, every marketing push, we were around the bonfire together bringing our unique creativity for a unified purpose. In the midst of this season, I began writing the second book, *Secrets of the Highlands*. For months, every weekend I was on the road signing books and meeting readers. Then every night between nine and midnight, I walked the road to Emmaus with Presence and Revelation.

It was humbling. It was inspiring. It was brutal.

Momentum seemed to be on our side. *Publishers Weekly* and *Writer's Digest* featured *Hunt for Eden's Star* prominently. We quickly reached top-ten lists on Amazon and even hit number one on Amazon Hot New Releases. The tour with Barnes & Noble launched the series. Interviews. Podcasts. Visits to middle schools and high schools. Everything happened so quickly that we didn't realize we were in the wild racing toward the Red Sea.

Not everyone was willing to create around the bonfire, which led to being disillusioned, disheartened, and disappointed. Pieces of the puzzle were never on the board, which left empty spaces around the fire. You can't force others to play in the wild if they're not willing to create in community. Sometimes you might be around the bonfire with only Presence and Revelation, and other times there's not an empty seat when egos, self-ambition, and pride are set aside.

I had a choice to make: Be frustrated by the detour or dig deeper. No doubt, I'd rather create with those around the bonfire than compromise calling. Sometimes the only way toward a divine appointment is through a sacred detour.

The Samaritan woman is a perfect example.

Most Jews avoided Samaria, but Jesus chose that route not because it was more efficient but because He was being intentional. Under the noon sun, He met a woman at the well whom everyone else avoided. A detour in geography became a collision of grace and truth. Jesus didn't elevate Himself; He lowered Himself by asking her for a drink. He welcomed a conversation that shame had once silenced. And from a place of humility and honesty, transformation began. The Samaritan woman ran back to her town and became one of the first messengers of the gospel.

But here's what I know about me: I'm not Jesus.

When the detour happened in the rollout of the *Beacon Hill* series, and I stood at the Red Sea waiting for it to part, my first response wasn't humility. Instead of a collision of grace and truth, my temptation was fire and brimstone. Everyone had sacrificed so much, given of their creativity, brought their craft around the bonfire because of relationships, all because they believed in the series. All had rolled up their sleeves and grabbed a shovel. But it was difficult to shovel while others stood by and watched. Presence whispered to me a thousand times that I was called to write this series no matter who stood against us.

Sometimes the sacred detour isn't for us—it's for the ones we'll meet along the way. The student in a classroom. The reader in a store. The scroller on social. The client in need of our craft. The email or DM from someone impacted by our creativity. These sacred detours dismantle hierarchy and make room for redemption.

Through my friend Jaime, I had the privilege of meeting Chip and Angi Nicholas. When Chip had been in his teens, his dad had died of a heart aneurism even as Chip performed CPR. His dad was only forty-eight. Chip knew this was an underlying possibility for him too. From marriage to kids and through the seasons of life, Chip and Angi learned more and more about holistic and natural ways to maintain heart health. Twenty-five years of meal planning and careful grocery shopping meant it was always on Angi's mind.

Early one morning, Chip woke up with what felt like a heart attack. It started as a shoulder pain but quickly moved into his chest. He took himself to the ER, only a few blocks from their home, while Angi stayed with their children. Weeks earlier, he'd had a physical exam, and there had been no sign of an aneurism. The doctor ordered a CT scan, and the results revealed a large mass. Chip was only forty-five. He immediately texted Angi, and the doctors set a plan in motion.

For two weeks, Chip and Angi waited for the surgery date. At any moment, the aneurism could burst, and he likely wouldn't survive. During those days of uncertainty, Angi handed him a copy of *Hunt for Eden's Star*, and he dove straight into the world of *Beacon Hill*. Angi later told me that in their twenty-five years together, she'd never seen him read fiction for fun, and this story had come to them in perfect timing. Battling. Persevering. Trusting. But what they didn't know at the time was that the mass had grown.

On the day of the surgery, there was even more news: a defective valve. While Chip was cracked open, Angi made the decision for doctors to insert a mechanical valve, which would last forever. To everyone's relief after much prayer, the surgery was a success. Chip returned home and began his road to recovery. He dove deeper into the *Beacon Hill* series, and it was a welcome sight for Angi during those months.

I was struck by Chip and Angi's story as a reminder of the power of redemption. Chip had lived for decades with the possibility of an aneurism. But Presence redeemed those years by giving Chip new life. When I visited with them over Zoom, I was humbled to hear how *Beacon Hill* offered him an escape from the uncertainty before the surgery and hope during the recovery. It was redemption for those moments when discouragement left me wondering if the series had really made a lasting difference. Now Chip and Angi are not only readers of my creativity, they're fellow wanderers around the bonfire in the wild.

When I peer in the rearview of *Beacon Hill*, all the way through the releases of *Secrets of the Highlands* and *Battle of Lion Rock*, I'm grateful for the breakthroughs, the encounters with readers who were impacted by the series, the creative collaborations, and witnessing the seed grow from beneath the soil into a beautiful Joshua tree. But honestly, even now, the missing spaces around the bonfire still sting and leave a slightly bitter taste.

In the margins, sacred detours have taught me the art of building bonfires, not pedestals. I've witnessed firsthand the aftermath when creatives and leaders place themselves above others. I've also experienced when neither will come to the bonfire because they're afraid of being held accountable. Instead, they climb onto their pedestal to protect themselves. Sometimes only Revelation can bring redemption in those wilderness seasons.

On the road to Emmaus, with the Samaritan woman at the well, and in the testimony of Chip and Angi, Revelation slows down, draws near, and creates space. The holy interruptions—the detours—become the very places where eyes are opened and lives are restored. No matter the outcome, we can choose between isolation and invitation, ego and empathy, spotlight or shared vision. Detours are where Kingdom collaboration begins—where we stop climbing and start creating around the bonfire together.

Wandering in the margins has guided me to make space for others, even when the path shifts away from where I expected. These days, I'm more drawn to building bonfires than pedestals. I'm less interested in stories of perfection. I'm less patient with leaders and creatives who place themselves and their righteous calling above others. And I'm more intrigued with grace, hope, and love found in conversations and creativity around the fire.

In many ways, this is the very reason I'm writing *Art of the Margins*: to be a small part of inspiring creatives, no matter where they might be, to keep walking toward the edge of brave. To honor the voices who come alongside, those who bring perspective and truth, even when it disrupts our rhythm. And to welcome the privilege of spending time around bonfires to encourage others along their journey in the margins.

> In their hearts humans plan their course, but the LORD establishes their steps. (Prov. 16:9 NIV)

Some of our most sacred creative moments come from what we don't plan: the unexpected ideas that surface in solitude, the reactions that initially sting but later forge an even stronger resilience. Like Revelation's detour through

Samaria, those interruptions become divine appointments—moments of transformation to shape our souls when we return to awe.

For those who lead, building bonfires sounds more daunting than climbing on pedestals. But when we inspire others to follow our vision, we have a responsibility to embrace their unique calling, not only our own. When we create alongside others, we must remain in a posture of being present to serve a greater mission and vision. Too often, we've seen leaders who place themselves on a pedestal and get knocked off. No one is there to pick them up, because everyone is gone. Leaders must earn their place around the bonfire; it's not simply reserved in a title.

> Love from the center of who you are; don't fake it. Run for dear life from evil; hold on for dear life to good. Be good friends who love deeply; practice playing second fiddle. (Rom. 12:10)

In the margins, we are challenged to embrace the art of remaining in awe of how creativity still flows through us even after disappointment, delay, or disillusionment. Our craft will stretch us beyond the edge of brave and remind us that our calling doesn't always guarantee clarity in the wild, but it does promise Presence. Our story was never meant to be built on a pedestal—it's always been about finding a seat around the bonfire. You see, sacred detours aren't distractions or dead ends from our calling: They're the way our calling in the margins is fulfilled.

23

RISK THE YES AGAIN

The air was thick with certainty from people convinced they knew where honor was seated. Men spoke confidently in a packed room, relaxing at the table as if belonging were a birthright. Reputation carried weight here. Then she walked in.

Her past came first—the glances, the labels, the whispered stories. In her hands, she carried an alabaster jar: sealed, costly, fragile. The kind of treasure one saved for the future. The kind of treasure you break only if you never intend to go back.

Interesting how this scene is bookended by the high priests and religious leaders meeting in secret to conspire about seizing and killing Jesus, and Judas Iscariot going to the cabal of high priests and asking how much they'd give him to hand the Messiah over (see Matt. 26:3–16).

In the center of this moment in history is the woman. She didn't ask permission. She crossed the room, fell at the feet of Jesus, and broke the jar. Not *opened*. Not portioned. Broken. Oil poured. Fragrance rose. An aroma settled into garments, walls, breath. No one could avoid inhaling her offering. But the criticism was fast and furious.

> That's criminal! This could have been sold for a lot and the money handed out to the poor. (Matt. 26:8b–9)

Surprisingly, the men who chastised the woman were Jesus' disciples. Stop for a second and think about that: Those who walked with Jesus, witnessed miracles, and learned from His teachings were swiftest to judge. Their opinion was that the oil was wasted, the oil could've been used differently, and the woman was careless because she didn't appreciate its value. Jesus was quick to step in:

> Why are you giving this woman a hard time? She has just done something wonderfully significant for me.... When she

> poured this perfume on my body, what she really did was anoint me for burial. You can be sure that wherever in the whole world the Message is preached, what she has just done is going to be remembered and admired. (Matt. 26:10b, 12–13)

Extravagant devotion confronted controlled religion. The yes that cost something exposed the safe offerings of those who gave only what was convenient. Jesus anticipated the days ahead, and the woman in her own pain and insecurity had given her very best. Her creativity, her risk to offend, was given in a moment when the cost of His sacrifice was real. In return, her offering was not judged by efficiency ... it was judged by love.

An offering that costs nothing changes nothing. An offering that costs everything changes the one who gives. The fragrance of the woman's yes did not fade. It traveled. It became a story told in every generation. When we risk the yes, even against the ridicule and judgment of others, we choose not to fade away. We wander deeper in the wild, offering the fragrance of our craft to Presence. We fall on our knees and dig creative ditches until we uncover a freshness to our gifts. The oil of our calling rises and a sweet aroma pierces our souls as we offer our very best.

Thousands of years later, Presence tuned Chris Harris's ear to recognize a familiar fragrance in unexpected places. Before studios and producing, before helping carry songs that would become altar calls for entire generations, Chris learned to listen while on the road with Michael W. Smith. Three weeks into a new season of calling, he stepped onto the stage of the Friends and Big Picture tours. Three years of nights when music and Presence were indistinguishable.

These weren't concerts or entertainment; they were authentic encounters. Rooms turned into altars. Sound turned into surrender. Heaven leaned in close. Those nights didn't just sharpen Chris's craft; they trained his ear and his soul. He learned to wait when the Spirit rested, to move when the moment opened, to protect what could not be manufactured. He learned how worship is not sound; worship is surrender.

Chris's wilderness journey led him to ForeFront Records and three students from Liberty University. No agenda. Just community. DC Talk was forming a voice with no category, no guardrails, no barriers, no rule book, and no formulas. They were free to create, to offer their most valuable creativity.

When Chris and his brother-in-law, Mark Heimermann, a three-time Grammy Award–winning record producer as well as an ASCAP Songwriter of the Year, stepped in to produce and develop DC Talk's self-titled debut in a house near Music Row, there was a special offering unrecognized in the moment.

Chris, Mark, Toby, Kevin, and Michael didn't press their sound into a mold; instead, they gathered around the bonfire to create an original. From the albums *Nu Thang* to *Free at Last* to *Jesus Freak* to *Supernatural*, Chris and Mark guided the trio to where Presence was growing fresh seeds of creativity beneath the soil. Those creative sessions were holy ground—open, risky, and true—during this season in the wild.

Out of the collaboration came "Red Letters" from the *Supernatural* album. Chris was an integral voice in bringing the song to life as one of the cowriters. It wasn't just a melody; it was Scripture as an encounter. It was a fragrant offering that elevated devotion over religious rules.

Dirt beneath our feet shifts as the words of Revelation become voice, grace becomes collision, and life wakes from the inside. I remember blasting "Red Letters" and the entire *Supernatural* album. It's still a reminder of why we say yes: to keep our sights and our hearts centered on what's true.

Chris chose to say yes to risk again. His journey in the wild brought him to seasons of wandering through studios and shaping songs of modern Christian music—not as a list of credits but as a lived presence. Decades behind consoles, in vocal booths, and in green rooms with fellow wanderers including Amy

Grant, Steven Curtis Chapman, Michael W. Smith, Jaci Velasquez, Rich Mullins, CeCe Winans, and many others. He didn't collect names as trophies; he carried moments around the bonfires with friends, stewarding presence, protecting craft, and releasing Revelation's creativity. And the fragrance traveled even further.

After a concert one night, a woman handed CeCe Winans a cassette. It was an unpolished demo—a husband plunking on a piano and a wife singing a song that felt like a prayer. But when CeCe listened to the lyrics and melody, she sensed the anointing oil. She called Chris, and they got together to hear the song in its rough state. It would've been easy to dismiss, but instead, Chris and CeCe leaned in a bit more.

"What would you need to produce this song?" CeCe asked.

"A fifty-piece orchestra," he replied.

"Okay," she answered.

No budgeting grid. No marketing plan. Just yes ... again.

Chris produced half of CeCe's *Alabaster Box* album, and Fred Hammond produced the other half. Two unique expressions of creativity. One fragrance. And the title track, "Alabaster Box," didn't merely recount the story of the woman who offered her very best—it carried it into eternity. Her offering became a voice for another woman's yes, across time.

The jar broke again. The room filled again.

I met Chris for the first time a few years after the release of *Alabaster Box*, but I've long known the story. Our years of friendship and seasons of working together have remained a bright light. We produced the *Break Through: Live at Saddleback* record—a night saturated in Presence where silence and celebration were an outpouring of reverence. When we stepped into Studio A at Capitol Records to produce a new artist, a familiar bond of friendship created one of the most fun creative experiences I've ever been part of. And the visits in Nashville, when we stayed up late in his living room sharing stories after midnight, are treasured.

Chris isn't just a producer. He is a listener—to Presence, to others, to atmosphere, to the tremble before worship becomes sound. Beyond his gifting, he's a dear friend to many. He's steady in the trenches, faithful in the in-between, present when calling weighs more than words can carry. He's someone you need around the bonfire.

On my journey in the margins, there were moments when I questioned whether I was willing to say yes to the risk again. During one of those seasons, I flew out to Nashville to finish a record Chris and I were working on. Uncertainty swirled around my next steps. Big risks were forced on me, and the weight was crushing. There was an underlying fear it was all going to crash into a million pieces. Those days working with Chris in the studio, then hanging out with him and Jan in their home, brought me a welcome and much-needed peace.

In the margins, we'll encounter seasons when all we can do is be present. Along our journey in the wild, we sit around the bonfire with fellow wanderers. Seasons when bonds are forged and healing is an outpouring of creativity's flow. We are encouraged to say yes in the chaos and not wait for the calm, when comfort dies so calling can live.

Years later, I was reminded of the creative bonfires with Chris as I reached a crossroads after the *Beacon Hill* trilogy. In the margins, there were mountaintops and valleys along the journey. There was a sense of accomplishment but also disappointment. I'm a gamer. I'm a fighter. I'm a wanderer in the wild. But this time, I wasn't sure I was ready to risk the yes again. I just wanted to sit around the bonfire for a while.

Years of world building, prayer, wrestle, wonder, and awe were poured onto those pages. After the book tours ended and the third book released, exhaustion left me slumped over instead of offering me a gentle landing. Honestly, I couldn't have pushed any harder. I thought the jar was empty. I mistook completion for conclusion. Seated around the bonfire, the margins revealed calling doesn't end when hands are empty: Calling, craft, creativity begin again when we pour ourselves out to Presence.

Then came the whisper.

"Tell the story behind the stories. Write from the margins ... again."

A piece of me paused, because I knew there'd be a cost to diving deeper in the wild. This yes wouldn't ask for imaginary worlds; it would ask for the realness of the margins. Not world building, but Revelation. Not distance, but surrender. Not an epic fantasy, but another blank page. Again, the cursor blinked like a heartbeat. A familiar friend sat beside me around the bonfire—Creativity. I heard the whisper again: "Break the jar."

Embracing the art of the margins is the breaking, the oil, the offering. Not because we understand, not because we're worthy, but because He speaks. Our obedience doesn't wait for certainty; it moves through the wilderness in conviction. "Master, we've worked hard all night and haven't caught anything. But because you say so, I will let down the nets" (Luke 5:5 NIV).

There is a jar in your hands.

You know exactly what it is. A calling you've delayed. A story you've kept quiet. A gift you've hidden for when it's safer. A dream you've over-prepared with a lingering fear. You're standing on the edge of brave, and the next step seems impossible. You've experienced the mountaintop, but you're wandering in the valley unsure of whether you have the courage to risk the yes again. What would happen if you broke the jar?

Long before the woman with the alabaster jar, there was another who whispered yes. Mary didn't receive a plan; she received a calling. Gabriel's words came without warning, without timelines, without explanation. And still she answered: "I am the Lord's servant.... May your word to me be fulfilled" (Luke 1:38 NIV).

Mary obeyed without fully understanding. She worshipped without controlling. She offered a whispered yes to the greatest miracle of the universe. She might've been afraid, but she said yes to the risk anyway. And we've seen this throughout history. The early church carried that yes into the streets, courts, and prisons. They proclaimed the Messiah publicly, even when safety would have counseled silence. We've seen in recent world events that the same is true today. Bold yeses create movements and revolutions, because revival begins on the far side of risk.

So why do we hesitate? The wisdom of hesitation sounds holy, though the one who hesitates may starve in the wilderness. No more ditches are dug. No more seeds are planted. No more harvests are reaped. "Whoever watches the wind will not plant; whoever looks at the clouds will not reap" (Eccl. 11:4 NIV). When we risk the yes again, we stop watching the wind and dig deeper than ever before.

Today is the day when comfort must die so calling can live. Break the jar. Pour the oil. Say yes when it costs you. Say yes when no one understands. Say yes when your voice shakes. Say yes when your bones tremble. Say yes in the chaos. Your yes is the fragrance Presence intends to release for someone else's freedom. A step beyond the edge of brave where awakening in your creativity begins and a revolution ignites holy fire deeper in the wild. Presence and Revelation are gathered around the bonfire. Now ... go. Break the jar. And change the world.

24

THE CREATIVE COST

Beside the ocean on the island of Marinduque in the Philippines, we climbed onto the back of a jeepney and headed straight into the heart of the province. We were on the hunt for a drum kit, fighting against the clock as we searched door to door. After hours of being pointed toward one barrio after another, we finally arrived at a run-down bar where we found the only drum kit on the entire island.

We paid cash to rent the kit, which had clearly lived a rough life. Rusted hardware. Dented cymbals. A stand that seemed to be held together by hope and a prayer. But we didn't need perfect—we just needed the basics. We also had a legendary drummer with us who could play anything, so I was confident it would work out.

In the center of town, we set up a simple audio rig: a microphone, guitar amps, a few wedge speakers, and the vintage kit. Children raced excitedly between plastic chairs while adults gathered before the last bit of light was swallowed up by the night. Not all of our concerts were in soccer fields or arenas. We knew we were going to a remote island, and the impromptu outdoor concert wasn't out of the ordinary. After dark, a crowd gathered as the music echoed through staticky speakers. I stood off to the side, breathing a sigh of relief that we'd found the impossible.

I never expected to be called into action.

Creativity has a way of asking me to improvise in the wild. A few songs into the set, in mid-chorus, the cymbal stand surrendered after a precision strike. With a loud crash, the cymbal and stand fell over like a tired old man collapsing without warning. While the music continued, our drummer glanced over at me as he kept the rhythm in sync. Before I had a second to think, I was racing across the small stage.

Not singing. Not speaking. Not playing.

I grabbed the cymbal stand and placed it where it had been moments earlier. Kneeling beside the drummer, I gripped the stand tight as the groove intensified. Fingers wrapped around the rusted metal, shoulders braced, sweat dripped. Every time he hit the cymbal, the crash rattled my skull. But I never let go, knowing the stand would surrender again. My ears rang so loud I couldn't tell the difference between the music and the crowd singing.

For the rest of the concert, I remained in that exact spot. And when the last song ended, no one offered me a standing ovation. I did get a high five from our drummer, though. Everyone seemed to have forgotten the cymbal stand was toast early on. But I'm convinced this was a moment when creativity happened.

Because creativity isn't about the spotlight. It's not even just about the expression. It's about showing up and supporting not only our creativity but the creativity of others. Especially when it would be easier to step away or stand on the sidelines. That is where the cost first appears: not in the big moments of inspiration, but in the quiet, unseen places where we choose to stay rooted. And sometimes amidst the noise of a crashing cymbal.

Marinduque flashed in my mind as I remembered the early days of the *Beacon Hill* book tour. A crashing cymbal might've been symbolic of the first date when I didn't sell out. A twinge of disappointment left me leery of what was ahead. As the dates mounted, I'd arrive at Barnes & Noble even more nervous and dreading the possibility of no sales. In each store, my gaze locked in on the stack of books waiting for me at the author table. After all the effort to pour my heart and soul into this story, there was enormous pressure to deliver.

I'd experienced author signings in the past where only a handful of people showed any interest. Most authors can relate to this part of the writer life. So, I was well aware of the impossible task ahead. In a way, it would've been easier to grip a cymbal stand or direct from behind a camera or console than to sit behind a stack of books. Before the second date on the tour, a voice within shouted, "Rejection is a reflection of your creativity." But I was also reminded of how Presence showed up that morning at the writers' conference in Colorado when my fear of public speaking faded and never returned.

The creative cost always involves risk. Risk of failure. Risk of rejection. Risk of disappointment. Risk of our craft crashing into oblivion.

I'd wandered in the wild over long seasons of creativity. I wasn't afraid to get burned, as those seasons forged a resilience and determination to charge forward. Yes, I'd prepared myself for the stacks of books being left behind. But I'd also imagined those books vanishing, going home with excited readers, even when my confidence wavered. Presence had entrusted me with this series, and this was a threshold that needed to be crossed.

I fought against any temptation to root success in the center of the page. Rather, I pushed toward the edges—the margins—to sense where Presence and Revelation waited in the wild. That's where faith was fire. That's where doubt was determination. That's where weakness was crushed by courage.

Driving to the second tour date, there was a choice to make: Expect the worst or pray for favor. Sit quietly at the table or engage with others. Keep the characters hidden on the page or share confidently about the world of *Beacon Hill*.

Before the second signing was over, all the books had been sold. This was the first time that ever happened to me. A flicker of hope sparked in my soul.

With each stop on the tour, the books continued to sell out, which garnered the attention of store buyers, who shared their experience with the next store on the tour. One sellout. Two sellouts. A wave formed, crested beautifully, and crashed in a powerful way. Some stores even sold out within the first hour. Others required me to stretch beyond comfort to share about the series. And as the sellouts mounted, the stacks of books at each store grew higher.

Ten sellouts. Fifteen sellouts. Twenty sellouts. Nearly thirty sellouts.

My courage overcame my introverted tendency, and I began to enjoy the signings rather than dread them. Believe me, I didn't sit back and watch the wind or stare at the clouds. Presence expected me to step out in faith and work hard. Even more important than the sales was what Presence and Revelation were forging in my soul.

When the tour brought me to Arizona, we had booked four author signings at Barnes & Noble stores within a twenty-four-hour period. In one of the higher-end stores, I even witnessed a flash mob race in and shoplift. My initial reaction was to hand them stacks of books on their way out to help with sales. But seriously, I was convinced this store would break my double-digit streak of sellouts. After the signing, there were books left over. Yet, several days later I received an email from a reader informing me the store had sold out of the books.

No one was more shocked than me.

While this was far from a world tour or dancing on the bestseller list, it was a reminder of what I was learning through the art of the margins. I was well aware that what was happening was an outpouring of planting, digging, watering, and believing for a harvest. It wasn't a master marketing plan. It was the favor of Presence from one store to the next. Now, it wasn't without persistence and a bit of pain, but I recognized the pillar of fire in the night sky.

Revelation once told a story about servants who were entrusted with talents: gifts, opportunities, seeds of possibility. Two servants took what they had and did something with it. They risked. They stretched. They acted. But one servant buried his gift in the ground—not out of laziness, but out of fear of getting it wrong or fear of being seen as a failure. He failed to steward well because he was afraid what was required of him was more than he could give.

> The master was furious. "That's a terrible way to live! It's criminal to live cautiously like that! If you knew I was after the best, why did you do less than the least?" (Matt. 25:26)

Creativity will cost before the soil bears fruit. When we choose to honor and nurture the craft Presence has placed in us, not everything we create will land. Not every attempt will matter in the way we'd hoped. Some ideas will take root and gain momentum. Some are met with silence. Some are halted in resistance. Some may never make it past the first step.

We plant without promise. We offer without guarantees. We hold nothing back ... and control nothing in return. And when something does begin to grow, it might not look impressive at first glance. But that doesn't mean a harvest isn't ready to break through the soil.

Revelation described the planting beautifully: a sower flinging seed with open hands, not calculating where it will grow but trusting the seeds would take root. He compared the Kingdom of heaven to a mustard seed—so small it could fall through our fingers without noticing. Yet inside that seed is the potential to become shelter, shade, bonfires, home.

Creative beginnings are oftentimes small in the same way. Not dramatic. Not celebrated. Not obvious. Not sellouts. Like a cymbal stand being held in place while onlookers remained focused on the music, not the one kneeling beside an instrument.

In truth, the first tour date for *Beacon Hill* should've been forgettable. But I'll always remember the one that didn't sell out. Not as a way to torture myself, but as a way to honor what Presence did in the months and years afterward. Readers were engaged. Growth was slow but steady. The journey required patience and trust in the wild. And it required endurance forged in my soul with a willingness to diligently nurture a dream.

By the time the tour ended, the experience wasn't about the books sold but about the lives who joined me around the bonfire. Creativity had a cost, but the reward was community. Even when the excitement wore off and the resistance rose like the Deeping Wall at Helm's Deep, the nurturing of my calling continued to keep the dream and message of *Beacon Hill* alive.

The dream is free—but the nurturing will cost us.

Creativity demands time when we're tired. Focus when we're stretched thin. Faith when we can't see the fruit. Endurance when we face rejection. Discipline when all we can hear is silence. Patience when our boots sink deeper in the sands of delay. Courage when self-doubt echoes in the wild. Determination when our work is misunderstood. Resilience when it's ignored. And sometimes replanting when it's celebrated too quickly before the roots have grown deep.

I've lived the dream when deals were inked—where everything aligned and the momentum seemed unstoppable. And I've walked away from dreams when everything was torched and left in ash, all in a single sentence. Both will shape and nurture you. It will not always be easy and pain free. There will be seasons when the cost will push us to the brink and not everything we create will be celebrated. We will experience rejection and maybe even ridicule. But everything we carry with honor—every seed we tend, every work we build—will shape us.

Paul wrote:

> Do your best. Work from the heart for your real Master, for God, confident that you'll get paid in full when you come into your inheritance. Keep in mind always that the ultimate Master you're serving is Christ. (Col. 3:23–24)

Revelation, the master storyteller, shared about two houses, two foundations, one storm. One house was built on solid rock, and the other on sinking sand. When rain poured down, the river flooded, and a tornado ripped through, but nothing moved the house built on the rock. When a storm raged and rolled in with strong waves, the house built on the sand collapsed.

Success and collapse look identical … until the waters rise.

It's only then we learn what held the structure up.

The same is true as wanderers in the wild. On the surface, we share similarities, but beneath the soil, the strength of our roots is tested. If our foundation is applause, the storm will take everything. If our foundation is identity built on achievement, we will sink when the wilderness seasons shift. If our ambition is to get *paid in full* in this world at all costs, ignoring the inheritance awaiting us in heaven, we will be washed away. But if our work is anchored in calling—in Presence, Revelation, Wonder, Creativity—the storm will strengthen us with clarity.

Sometimes clarity is revealed in humor.

Like the day I was signing books and a woman asked for a copy to encourage her teenage son's friend, who was going through a difficult season. I'm not sure what came over me, but I decided I was going to write a Scripture beneath my signature. I wanted to be pastoral. After all, I was a missionary kid, a seasoned ministry leader, a faith-filled entrepreneur, and an author, so this should've been quick and easy. Thoughtful. Meaningful. So, I wrote the Scripture reference as Exodus 12:12—instead of Exodus 14:14.

Later, when I was seated in a green room, I began wondering about the Scripture reference. *Did I write down the right one?* I wanted the Scripture to encourage this teenager who was struggling. I searched Bible Gateway for both passages. First, I opened Exodus 14:14: "The LORD will fight for you; you need only to be still" (NIV). That was the passage. Rock solid. Alone in the room, it hit me: *I wrote down the wrong one.* Uh-oh—sand. I looked up Exodus 12:12 and stopped cold:

> On that same night I will pass through Egypt and strike down every firstborn of both people and animals, and I will bring judgment on all the gods of Egypt. I am the LORD. (Ex. 12:12 NIV)

At that moment, I might've said a few words under my breath as panic punched me in the chest. Not exactly the inspiration I was hoping to share. The wave crashed on my house.

We launched a full-scale mission through the building to find the autographed book before it disappeared and ruined a young teenager's life. Fortunately, we found the book, and I signed a new one, avoiding a catastrophe.

Everyone lived to tell the story. But the moment struck me because creativity or any shred of success will humble you, especially if you're convinced your house is rock solid. It will bring you to your knees—not just in worship, but in laughter at your own humanity.

The creative cost will challenge us not just to build but also to remain steadfast. Our craft and calling are sustained in the roots of the vine. They're sustained by Presence, not performance. By staying in relationship with Revelation, not striving to rely on our own gifts. By watering the soil of our creativity until the branches grow fruit. We are the branches, held by Presence who began the work in the first place.

And this brings me back to that night in Marinduque. To the cymbal stand in my hands. To the ringing in my ears. To the moment no one saw. I didn't understand it then, but I do now.

Sometimes the most creative act we can do is to simply stay around the bonfire long enough for growth to occur. Creativity is not the moment of applause. It is the long obedience that comes in the seasons before. It is the willingness to hold the small things with an open hand, faithfully, while Presence grows our seeds into beautiful trees and builds our souls firmly on the rock.

The *Beacon Hill* tour was a lesson in obedience that I will carry through my life. When the momentum shifted and the story reached beyond, I was reminded the cost of creativity is real. But so is the formation. So is the fruit. So are Presence and Revelation, who remained with me through it all.

Our souls are forged in the process. Maybe the most sacred creative ditches are the ones we surrender—the ones where we've poured out our souls in sacrifice. Maybe that's where the real creativity begins.

25

GUARD YOUR CREATIVE FIRE

Waves crashed against a weathered pier as gusts of wind whisked all around. I pulled my hoodie tight against the bitter, stinging cold as my gaze locked on the beauty of Presence in all His might and splendor. There's something about standing in the center of nature that grounds us. Something about the magnificence of the world being spoken into existence that should make us not fear or worry about anything—and yet we do.

Each set of enormous waves roared powerfully toward shore, a reminder of projects in the rearview. My creative fire was burning, but not as bright as it once did. Another stretch grinding through a rigorous production schedule, as well as writing two novels within the same period, left me reaching for the ropes.

I'd made it to the twelfth round, bloodied and beaten but still standing. I'd survived a challenging and grueling season in the wilderness where sand was relentless and stone was breathtaking. As each wave slammed against the shore, I exhaled just a bit more. I'd been digging creative ditches for a long time, so I recognized my tendency to push beyond the limits. When burnout bared its fangs, there was a choice: Fight my way to the bell or stand still in the margins and listen for the whisper of Presence.

My imagination fired on overdrive as I walked across the pier. Creativity wasn't something I could turn off and on. Even when I didn't feel inspired, stories lingered within reach. In the darkest moments, in the silence of exhaustion, a spark of inspiration might strike. I'd found inspiration in the valleys of discouragement and staked milestones of creativity on rocky summits. But on this day, the story playing in my mind resisted fading to black.

Was I ready to face another blank page? I knew there'd be a cost. There had always been. But this time, I wasn't sure. I was more seasoned and scarred than when I'd climbed into the VW Bug years earlier. Back then, I was wide-eyed and ready to conquer the world. But there were seasons since which challenged my resilience. Some were traveled with only a few, and others alongside fellow wanderers around bonfires. I'd grown to recognize my tendencies, so when burnout wrapped around my soul, the battle to guard my creativity began.

In a perfect world, I'd dive in with total faith and chase the story to the last page. But this time, a gentle whisper urged me to pause. Presence was guarding my creative fire ... because I wasn't. Inhale. Dream. Exhale.

One block from the pier, the rumbling waves faded amidst the peacefulness of a sleepy beach town. A perfect escape to recover and renew my calling. There was satisfaction in finishing the *Beacon Hill* series, but there was also unsettledness—a sting left me questioning whether I was willing to dig more ditches, plant more seeds, water more soil. I'd poured every ounce of my craft onto the page, and yet there were roots left dying beneath the vine.

Accountability yanked from the dirt was now buried somewhere else. Sacrifice ripped from the soil was tossed aside. Creativity grown from a seed of a dream sprouted branches of a nightmare. Truth stacked and lit on fire, burning the ashes of an epic adventure.

There were moments when I was angered by the unsettledness and battle scars left on my faith from this season in the wild. Presence stepped in and did what I was too burned out to do: New characters. New worlds. New plots. New series. Even though I wasn't ready, standing still in the margins was exactly where Presence wanted me so that I would listen.

> Keep vigilant watch over your heart; *that's* where life starts.... Keep your eyes straight ahead; ignore all sideshow distractions. Watch your step, and the road will stretch out smooth before you. Look neither right nor left; leave evil in the dust. (Prov. 4:23, 25–27, italics in original)

My brawler and survivor mentality wanted to throw down. Still, Presence urged me to guard and watch over my heart, no matter the outcome of any creative endeavor. But I was on edge, tempted to shout from the mountaintops until the world listened. The truth is, no matter how it was spun, there was no chance of changing minds and hearts as an aftermath followed me for a long time.

One of the most difficult decisions during this season was to keep my sights straight ahead and to root Exodus 14:14 in my soul: "The LORD will fight for you; you need only to be still" (NIV). It wasn't any easy choice. I didn't want to remain silent or watch my steps. I wanted the situation to be made right because I deserved it. But that's not what Presence was asking of me. The more injustice haunted my nightmares, the more I risked losing my calling, my craft, my creativity as a storyteller.

Strolling through this peaceful town, a battle waged in my spirit. "For this reason I remind you to fan into flame the gift of God, which is in you" (2 Tim. 1:6a NIV). "Better one handful with tranquility than two handfuls with toil and chasing after the wind" (Eccl. 4:6 NIV). Presence challenged me to make a choice: Fan the flame of the gift of calling with my weapon of creativity or chase after toil in the wind. The decision was clear, but it wasn't easy.

Creativity is sacred ... but fragile. It burns bright when fed but fades when neglected. The greatest threat to our creative fire isn't failure—it's anything that slowly smothers the spark. Fatigue disguised as hustle. Comparison marked as inspiration. Applause mistaken for calling. Disappointment camouflaged as righteousness. We stop guarding our creative fire when we're distracted right or left as the noise of this world smothers the flame.

We live in a culture addicted to noise, to movement, to trends. But fire doesn't thrive in chaos; it thrives in care. What fuels us is worth protecting. Our focus. Our rhythms. Our disciplines. Our joy. Our bonfires. These are not only where skills are forged, they're where survival rooted in resilience is found.

We don't just need inspiration to create; we need space to breathe and to be. We step back from the endless scroll to listen, to be refilled along our journey of striving amidst the weight to produce. When we guard our creative fire, we return to those places of obscurity where the flame was first lit. Because if we don't guard the fire, we'll lose the reason we started. But if we do guard it, our calling and creativity will burn through anything.

Days spent in this sleepy beach town offered me a chance to exhale. A reminder to protect what fueled me. A warning my creative fire wouldn't protect itself. I needed to feed it. I needed to protect it. I needed to steward it like it mattered—because it did. I'd ridden the waves of creativity over long seasons, but this was one of those moments when I needed to return to obscurity, to return to the rhythm of the margins for Presence to reignite my calling.

What do we do when our creative fire fades?

Nehemiah's story has always struck me as one of the clearest pictures of what it feels like to create something meaningful when the world keeps trying to tear it down. He wasn't scripting a book or a story. He was rebuilding a wall stone by stone, prayer by prayer, but the battle around him felt strangely familiar.

As soon as he began the work, the opposition gathered. Voices rose against him. Threats came. Doubt came. People tried to distract him, discourage him, intimidate him, and drag him away from the very thing Presence assigned him to do (see Neh. 4–6). Nehemiah wasn't just stacking stones—he was fighting to stay focused in the midst of relentless noise.

At one point, he told the people to build with a tool in one hand and a sword in the other (Neh. 4:17). Create and defend. Construct and protect. It's a rhythm every creative knows, even if we've never named it. Nehemiah reminds us the work itself may not be the hardest part. Sometimes the real challenge is guarding our fire when everything around us threatens to extinguish the flames.

In Exodus, Presence gives the priests a simple but powerful instruction:

> Now, order the Israelites to bring you pure, clear olive oil for light so that the lamps can be kept burning. In the Tent of Meeting, the area outside the curtain that veils The Testimony,

> Aaron and his sons will keep this light burning from evening until morning before GOD. (Ex. 27:20–21a)

Morning and night, they brought fresh oil and trimmed the wick so the flames kept shining inside the Tabernacle. It wasn't a one-time spark; it was a continual tending of the flames. The fire was holy, not because it was dramatic, but because it was faithful.

That picture stays with us. The priests were stewards of the environment that allowed the flames to burn bright. They protected the fire from neglect. They guarded it from the darkness. When I think about creativity, I see those flames.

Burnout doesn't happen because the fire disappears; it happens because we stop tending the flame. We pour out so much of ourselves in the work that we forget to refill what has been consumed in the lamp of our soul. The lamp reminds us the creative fire given by Presence is not self-sustaining. It needs rest. It needs space. It needs rhythms. It needs the quiet care of someone who understands its worth.

Holy fire doesn't stay lit on its own. It must be tended, protected, nourished. But there's another truth we can't ignore: Sometimes it's not just neglect that threatens the flame but the culture around us. While the priests show us the daily care of the fire, Daniel shows us how to protect the fire from shutting down.

> When Daniel learned that the decree had been signed and posted, he continued to pray just as he had always done. His house had windows in the upstairs that opened toward Jerusalem. Three times a day he knelt there in prayer, thanking and praising his God. (Dan. 6:10)

The decree was the forbiddance of prayer to anyone but the king. Breaking the decree to honor Presence meant Daniel received an all-expenses-paid vacation in the lion's den. Even the king didn't want Daniel to be harmed, but he was too afraid to break his own decree. "At daybreak the king got up and hurried to the lions' den. As he approached the den, he called out anxiously, 'Daniel, servant of the living God, has your God, whom you serve so loyally, saved you from the lions?'" (Dan. 6:19–20).

Imagine this on the big screen—with a Hans Zimmer soundtrack, thank you. The moment of truth. Dead or alive. "'O king, live forever!' said Daniel. 'My God sent his angel, who closed the mouths of the lions so that they would not hurt me'" (vv. 21–22a).

While the priests guarded the flame and oil with stewardship, Daniel guarded the fire in his soul with devotion and discipline. He didn't wait for inspiration. He didn't adjust his faith to conform to cultural pressure. He didn't allow fear to rewrite his rhythms. Three times a day, he returned to Presence—quiet, steady, consistent—tending the fire even when it could have cost him everything. He spent the night in the den of beasts and walked out without a scratch.

Guarding our creative fire isn't always a dramatic moment of breakthrough; oftentimes it's long and steady obedience in the margins. Nehemiah guarded the work, a reminder for us to protect our creativity and calling when the wilderness grows loud. The priests guarded the flame, reminding us to tend the fire with rest and rhythm. Daniel guarded the soul, a promise the fire is ultimately sustained by stubborn disciplines that anchor us in Presence.

When we choose to rebuild, to refill, to return, and to remain, the flame we thought was fading begins to burn again—steadier, stronger, and with a holy fire that comes only from creating in the margins and wandering free in the wild.

26

KEEP SHOWING UP

Many believe a myth that creativity is born only in inspiration, brilliance visits us in rare flashes, and greatness erupts in singular moments witnessed by culture. But the truth is less glamorous—and far more powerful. Creativity is born in persistence. Brilliance is forged in faithfulness. And greatness grows in the margins where no one is watching, even when we're stepping out of seasons when every ounce of calling is poured out in the real of the wild.

The margins become reality the moment real pushes back.

As wanderers of Presence, it's easier to believe when creativity flows. But the strength and resilience of our calling are proven in the tension between craft and reality. Some are stretched, others are exhausted, far too many remain unseen, and even the most gifted question whether their creativity matters.

When the blank page looks empty, the inspiration is quiet, or the story doesn't make sense, we feel we're sacrificing more than we have left. Fear whispers we're not good enough. Those moments are when faith in the margins becomes real. Those moments shape us. Those moments reveal us. Those moments are where brilliance begins—not the brilliance of genius, but the brilliance of light.

Leaders, artists, storytellers, musicians, teachers, builders, and dreamers till and water the soil when growth isn't visible. In the early mornings when everyone else is asleep. In the late-night sessions when melodies strike the right chords. In the silence when visions transform into visuals on a screen. In the margins, possibilities trump the odds, and the brilliance of light shines brighter when we just keep showing up.

Faithfulness is fuel to our creative fire. In the unseen moments—the hours alone with ideas, drafts, prayers, sketches, and uncertainty—we build an altar in the wild where Presence forms us. A place where the hidden grind isn't punishment but preparation for what's ahead. A place where our creative fire is protected as we become resilient, shaped, and forged in the margins. We gather around bonfires where our souls are strengthened and courage fuels our calling, where character is built to carry our creativity into eternity.

Culture sees a finished canvas as brilliance. Heaven sees the brushstrokes of everyday life. Reality pushes back against fresh breakthroughs, but breakthroughs don't come only to those who are brilliant. Breakthroughs come to those who refuse to quit. The art of the margins reveals that creativity is not a sprint; it's a journey in a vast wilderness. When we keep showing up, consistency creates momentum, momentum grows calling, and calling gives our creativity weight in the wild.

Momentum doesn't show up in the beginnings. In the margins, momentum grows from a thousand footsteps toward the edge of brave. Our quest for brilliance isn't about chasing genius; it's about pursuing the light that shines brighter when we create. We are not the ones who bring brilliance. Brilliance is a gift from Presence when we are faithful in the long obedience of our calling.

Oftentimes we believe our creativity is about what we produce. Through wilderness seasons, we learn a deeper truth resonates when calling shapes us while we shape the work. The discipline of showing up forges character and endurance that strengthen our souls. In obedience, we deepen our faith through standing in the fiery furnaces and lion dens of this world. We're not just creating a story: The story is creating us into who we are destined to be. That's where faith becomes real and true.

> So let's not allow ourselves to get fatigued doing good. At the right time we will harvest a good crop if we don't give up, or quit. (Gal. 6:9)

Creativity isn't truly tested on the mountaintop. Creativity is tested in the margins. When the dream feels heavy, the inspiration runs empty, the answers seem out of reach, the journey feels unfair, or when the calling costs more than we expected. That is where creativity and faith become real. Not the kind we talk about ... the kind we live. In the midst of wilderness seasons, we hold on to a promise: The harvest comes to the faithful.

Many of us need to be reminded of this more than once, maybe more than a thousand times. When creative endeavors reach the mountaintop, it's easy to talk a big game. Keep showing up. Just believe. Pray harder. Have more faith. But when those endeavors don't turn out the way we expected, or cost us more than we anticipated, it's not so easy to proclaim a harvest is coming. Honestly, it's easier to convince ourselves we'll be left wandering aimlessly in a desert without food or water. That's why creativity requires courage, because the real of the wild will challenge our faith again and again.

The question is not, Do we feel strong enough?

The question is, Will we have the courage to show up anyway?

Every creative hits the edge of the margins—the place where what we believe about Presence and Revelation collides with what we see in front of us. The edge is terrifying when we question whether the work matters. Maybe we misheard our calling. Maybe we've peaked. Maybe no one's interested in our gifts anymore. Maybe we've fallen behind in our craft. Maybe reality is what it is. But the edge of the margins is also where deeper faith and greater creativity are forged. The margins don't need geniuses; the margins need light. Sometimes the brilliance is simply refusing to walk away.

Creativity rarely reveals the ending from the beginning. It doesn't unfold like a map. It's written in faith when we don't always understand where the story is going, but we go anyway. Clarity in our calling rarely sharpens before commitment; it sharpens when we keep showing up. The fog lifts. The next step appears. Presence whispers direction. We sit. We listen. We release. We repeat. We don't need the full map. We grasp only the next moment in obedience.

This is the quiet rhythm of calling.

Showing up roots us in the rhythm as we stop chasing someone else's brilliance and shine in our own. In the purpose of Presence, we show up faithfully and stop looking sideways. We stop mimicking genius. We stop waiting for validation. We stop contorting ourselves into someone else's calling. We simply keep showing up ... because nothing Presence begins in our lives is random. No seed is wasted. No moment is insignificant. Acts of obedience become sparks of something greater when Presence shines His brilliance on the scattered seeds planted.

Chapters written after midnight. Emails sent after a rejection. Melodies hummed after a rehearsal. Pitches we thought went nowhere. Ideas we almost quit on from one negative word. A quiet yes whispered in the noise. Small steps taken in consistent faith.

Just show up.

Most wait for momentum before consistency, but consistency creates momentum. Not intensity. Not hype. Not genius. Consistency. The ones who endure know this truth. Momentum is built by returning, day after day, through ordinary faithfulness. Sustained discipline trusts Presence with the unseen hours as heaven multiplies what consistency surrenders.

We are not meant to carry yesterday's success or failure into today's calling. Lamentations 3:22–24 whispers, "GOD's loyal love couldn't have run out, his merciful love couldn't have dried up. They're created new every morning. How great your faithfulness! I'm sticking with GOD (I say it over and over). He's all I've got left."

Every morning is a resurrection of grace and mercy for the creative soul. We don't need to chase perfection. All we need is to be with Presence. He isn't asking for flawless—He's asking for surrender. Tomorrow will bring its own mercies. So will the day after that. And the day after that. All He asks is to keep showing up so His presence will meet us there.

The art of the margins leads us to creativity rooted in conviction as unseen works of brilliance. Where the unnoticed hours shape greater depth. Where seasons of obedience forge resilient strength. Where hidden sacrifices birth greater creativity. Remember, we're not just forming the work: The work is forming us. Discipline becomes devotion. Repetition becomes resilience. Endurance becomes the holy fire through every season. When we keep showing up, we become wanderers who carry the brilliance of Presence everywhere.

If you are in a wilderness season of exhaustion, wondering if it's working or questioning if the spark is still there, you are not alone. We've all been right where you are, and we are still standing. Those of us who have chased creativity in the margins wander through these seasons even now. But we've learned not to stay long. Instead, we've chosen to show up in the fog, the shadows, the uncertainty, believing there is more to discover in the wild.

When the story doesn't make sense or the blank page lingers ... those are the moments when brilliance stretches our faith. Even when we're carrying more than we want. Even when we feel unseen. We keep showing up, consistent in our calling and craft, as Presence strengthens our faith beyond our circumstance. This is the steadfastness Paul wrote about in 1 Corinthians 15:58: "With all this going for us, my dear, dear friends, stand your ground. And don't hold back. Throw yourselves into the work of the Master, confident that nothing you do for him is a waste of time or effort."

"Stand your ground" doesn't mean we never wobble. "Don't hold back" doesn't mean we never doubt. It means wobble and doubt don't determine direction. Exhaustion doesn't erase calling. Questions don't cancel obedience. Brilliance still shines in us and through us.

We throw ourselves into Revelation's work as the brilliance of Presence shines bright. We keep showing up in the silence, the doubts, the fog of our calling, to encounter breakthrough in our creativity. But it's not the breakthroughs that make our creativity brilliant; it's the shining light of Presence. In the margins, we learn that faith embraces discipline in obedience, because our future brilliance depends on it.

27

JUST DIG DITCHES

Near an oasis in the wild, countless ditches waited for seeds to be sown while a harvest grew from seeds already planted. Vines broke through the soil's crust near clusters of Joshua trees, their knobby limbs reaching toward the sky. Below the soil, the trees spread their fibrous root system deep. But go deeper and you'd discover an extensive world of roots searching for rivers.

Walk between the Joshua trees, and you'd sense Presence surrounding an oasis of creativity. Stories that were grown. Endeavors that were growing. Collaborations that had barely sprouted. Mounds of fresh dirt as proof of digging in obedience and discipline. Seasons watered in faith, in pain, in resilience, in brokenness, in awe and wonder.

> But blessed is the man who trusts me, GOD,
> the woman who sticks with GOD.
> They're like trees replanted in Eden,
> putting down roots near the rivers—
> never a worry through the hottest of summers,
> never dropping a leaf,
> serene and calm through droughts,
> bearing fresh fruit every season. (Jer. 17:7–8)

The promises of Presence are rooted in trust, but trust requires faith in the waiting of the unknown. Discipline moves us to replanting when serenity and calmness hand us a shovel. We return to the wild—the margins—in wilderness seasons to just dig ditches. Each shovel of dirt is an act of bravery. Each mound of soil is proof of courage. With each seed planted, hope and faith are forged in resilience. It's the work. It's the determination. It's the surrender. And deep beneath the soil where the river flows, it's the enduring strength in our calling.

Not perfection. Not success. Not failure.

Just obedience in the unseen places of the margins.

When I opened my eyes, the oasis vanished, though my soul remained in the margins. Around me, clear blue skies welcomed a brisk coastal morning and a peaceful ocean. On this day, the power of a raging sea settled into calmness as memories of milestones faded. To be still was a chance to remember, to reflect, and to pray for a revolution. I'd walked an unplanned path and survived in the wild. But it wasn't me who protected my soul, my craft, my calling. Presence guided every ditch and watered every inch of soil when I wasn't strong enough. He was the river running deep beneath the ground through droughts and harvests.

Mine is just one story. I never could've planned where Creativity has taken me, and I don't know where He will take me in the seasons ahead. I've tried to remain faithful in obedience. I haven't always been successful, but I haven't always failed. That's the beauty of the wild.

On the days when the skies are dark and the world is silent, the margins forge in us the determination to remain ditch diggers. When inspiration runs dry. When the soil is hard. Still we dig. We aren't made to wait for rain. We are made to unearth rivers—to dig and plant until heaven breaks through. What flows beneath the surface spreads beyond what grows above ground. Roots stretch wider than anyone will ever see ... to where real creativity and true calling flow as one.

In success, there will be temptations to dig the wrong ditches. We'll stand on stages and thirst for the applause. We'll sign deals that build bigger houses. We'll share highlight reels on social to validate brands. We'll paint on canvases to resemble the world instead of being an original. We'll trade seeds of calling for soils of commerce. We'll believe ditchdigging is the gift instead of what lies deeper. And we'll stop digging until heaven breaks through, relying on our strength and talent alone. Warning: All of it will leave us thirsty and starving in the wild.

Creativity isn't just about the art we make, the deals we strike, or the influence we gain: It's about Presence who walks with us. He is Creativity, who unearths the soil we are too weak to dig. He gives us the courage to keep wandering in the wilderness when there's no oasis in sight. And when we pick up a shovel to show up in dry and desolate seasons, we're saying we still believe that Presence, Creativity, Revelation—the Rivers of Life—flow through our souls. We keep digging not because it's easy, but because deeper ditches reach stronger rivers. And when seasons of drought come, we draw from the Rivers of Life as our lifeline.

The Rivers of Life offer us a gift beyond our imagination, our craft, our skills. We are invited into the beauty of an oasis to walk with Them along our earthly journey into eternity. No greater gift will ever be given. All we have to do is surrender ourselves, embrace our calling, and just dig ditches. We don't look back at the past. We don't look forward to the unseen. We simply gaze on the awe and wonder of now.

Many of us are still learning to bury our past success and failure to be free in awe and wonder. We hold on to moments when culture recognized our achievements. We allow failure to consume our minds long after the season is over. We relish success, and we dread that falling short will define our legacy. But those moments are fleeting and vanish in a blink. We spend seasons unable to let go of what's already done instead of searching for what's hidden beneath the soil.

We've allowed the past to define calling—success and failure. But Presence offers us a gift to bury it once and for all. To be free to create without expectation, restriction, limitation. Revelation encourages us to keep our sights on the path, not the horizon. To discover where our journey is leading us next, one step at a time toward the edge of brave.

New seasons of digging and watering the soil. New adventures in the wild. A new story brewing in a sleepy beach town. An escape from the world of supernatural fantasy. A detour from espionage thrillers. A welcome resurgence of storytelling. Another blank page. Yes, there's uncertainty. But there is also certainty the Rivers of Life remain roaring for eternity.

Some stories take time to reveal themselves, but the story playing in my imagination sprouted from the first page. There was an ease to the creative process. Characters were alive. Worlds seemed real. Story left me energized to keep writing. After seasons in the wilderness, I was stubbornly resilient in the pursuit of my craft, my calling. But creativity in the margins required digging deep enough to be rooted in the Rivers of Life.

Whenever we stop digging, we stop trusting the Rivers of Life flowing beneath the soil, and our souls wander further into a wasteland. We're distracted from our calling without the hype, the tour, the deals, the notoriety. Only the Rivers of Life can fill the emptiness of distraction in our creativity. All we're called to do is dig and plant until heaven breaks through. May this truth still resonate for all who have shown up when it was dry. Dig and plant. Everything else is a distraction—a sideshow.

In our oasis of creativity, we're challenged to dig deeper to catch a glimpse of the Rivers of Life flowing in our work, our lives, our craft, our gifts, our calling.

Isn't that what it's all about?

We're created to draw nearer to the Rivers of Life, closer to the promise of eternity. That's the story we're called to write. That's the masterpiece we're created to paint. That's the business we're called to build. That's the message we're called to share. The ways in which we communicate and express this truth are unique in our creativity. It may not look like Sunday morning. It might look like flipping a few tables. It might look like gathering around a bonfire to create in community. It might be creating alongside those who don't yet believe the margins are a place where we encounter His beauty.

In the margins, we are created to worship through our creativity. But we must choose which path will capture our souls. Will we surrender to the temptations of culture, or will our worship resonate in the Rivers of Life? One way is tainted; the other is pure.

To know for certain, just dig ditches.

28

DON'T RUSH THE REVEAL

One of my favorite chefs is Gordon Ramsay. Don't judge.

While you may not agree with Gordon's brash leadership style, colorful language, or relentless pursuit of excellence, you can't deny he has climbed to the summit of the culinary world. Imagine the years spent in kitchens where he wasn't the best, where he wasn't the polished Michelin star–rated chef on the shows, but the unknown cook sweating over hot stoves to express his creativity on a plate. He has not only strived for success in his creativity with mouthwatering dishes and as a successful entrepreneur, but he's also helped others reach their potential in the culinary world and beyond.

None of it was an overnight success.

I've always wondered what it'd be like to be a chef, but I'm a total mess in the kitchen. Give me a bottle of olive oil, and I'll make sure it splatters everywhere. Ask me to steam rice, and you'll get water boiling over and grains stuck to the bottom of the pot. Leave me alone to sear steak, and smoke is guaranteed to fill the kitchen.

But then a miracle happened: I bought my first air fryer, also known in our house as the *second wife*—named by the wife.

I was late to the air-fryer party, but the first time I powered it on, I swear I heard angels singing from on high. A total game changer. All of a sudden, I was a chef. Sort of. I cooked rib eyes, filet mignons, salmon, potatoes, steamed rice, sautéed vegetables, and even scrambled eggs. I was unstoppable ... as long as I followed the instructions, used the right temperature, and set the right time.

I'd stand in front of the air fryer as it was cooking, admiring the ease with which I was creating a delicious meal. It was easy. But let's be honest: It wasn't creative. There wasn't any skill involved. Push a few buttons and watch the magic happen. Perfect every single time. Funny enough, my daydream of becoming a chef shifted from sweating over a stove to watching the time count down on a machine.

We live in a culture addicted to instant. Fast food. Quick launches. Viral moments. Easy likes. Metrics now measure meaning, and speed is often mistaken for creative significance. But the most powerful creativity—the kind that reverberates long after the noise fades—is almost always forged slowly. In silence. In shadows. In places where no one's noticing.

I've watched countless cooking segments with Gordon and other chefs, and I have learned a few lessons. Wait for the perfect time to flip the steak. Don't open the oven too early with a soufflé. Know when to turn off the burner for the most amazing scrambled eggs. Do not rush developing depth of flavor.

Like the greatest chefs, we too are invited into the brave restraint of waiting.

In the margins, we embrace a holy tension between what we feel called to create and when it is truly ready to be seen. The process marinates the flavor of our creativity. The waiting shapes what we see on the plate. It reveals the visual—and the darkroom matters. The refining matters. The forming matters. Creativity is not an air fryer; it's a kiln. And what's forming in the dark shines brighter in the light ... if we let it finish.

We were created to reveal something sacred—shaped by time, tension, and trust. Premature exposure can kill what is still becoming. When we rip the seed out of the soil just to "see how it's doing," we stop it from taking root. Creativity works the same way. Vision works the same way. Voice works the same way. Calling works the same way.

Long before Jesus preached on hillsides, healed the sick, or turned the world right side up, He lived in complete obscurity. Thirty years hidden. Thirty years uncelebrated as the Messiah. Thirty years when nothing looked extraordinary from the outside. We get only one small glimpse of His childhood in Scripture—twelve-year-old Jesus in the temple—and then the story goes quiet for nearly two decades. No public miracles. No crowds. No ministry platform. No disciples. Just the Son of Presence living an ordinary life in a dusty, forgotten town.

But hidden doesn't mean inactive.

Silent doesn't mean stagnant.

Unseen doesn't mean unfinished.

Those thirty years weren't wasted; they were forming Him. Heaven entrusted Jesus with anonymity before entrusting Him with influence. Presence wasn't in a hurry: He was shaping His Son in the dark of this world. Jesus learned the rhythms of work. He wasn't in a synagogue all day; He was in a workshop. Sawdust in His hair. Calluses on His hands. He built things long before He began building the Kingdom. Creation taught Him patience. Craft taught Him care. Carpentry taught Him how every masterpiece takes time.

Luke wrote that "Jesus grew in wisdom and stature, and in favor with God and man" (Luke 2:52 NIV). He learned obedience in the ordinary. His growth required seasons. His favor required faithfulness. He didn't skip the process: He lived in the margins as the Son of Presence who was fully man.

Jesus learned the intimacy of being unseen. Before anyone knew His name, Presence said, "This is my Son, whom I love; with him I am well pleased" (Matt. 3:17b NIV). Jesus began His public ministry already approved. Already affirmed. Already beloved. And His life of compassion welcomed those seen as less than. He broke bread with those who didn't believe. He invited them to follow Him, because His love meant they were already approved, already affirmed, already beloved.

He lived as a seed in the soil. Hidden but germinating. Quiet but full of power. Unseen but preparing for the exact moment Presence would say, "Now."

And when His ministry finally began, He moved with authority, spoke with clarity, and carried a depth that couldn't have been air-fried. The hidden years do their work and teach us where our calling actually comes from. We are in this world, but we are not of this world.

We read the Gospels and see: "Jesus then appeared, arriving at the Jordan River from Galilee" (Matt. 3:13a). He didn't just appear—He arrived. There's a difference. We appear when we step out from obscurity, but we *arrive* when Presence releases us into our calling. Jesus wasn't rushing the reveal. He was trusting the timing of Presence.

That's an invitation for each one of us.

To stop panicking when creativity and calling feel slow. To stop assuming silence means failure. To stop believing that appearing is proof of calling. We don't know what Presence is doing in the unseen to prepare us for our arrival. If Revelation spent most of His earthly life in obscurity, then those seasons must be holy ground. The margins must have purpose. And the dark must be where Presence does His most essential work.

Years before the British handed Hong Kong back to the Chinese government, my dad traveled with a close friend into mainland China. They had opportunities to witness the underground churches long before many realized the roots of Christianity were spreading across the nation. What looked small from the outside was seismic in the dark. The actions we've seen in recent years offer evidence that when the reveal arrived, the world noticed ... and the Western church was challenged in a fresh way.

The same is true in our calling. Our art. Our leadership.

If we force the reveal, we get attention when we *appear.*

If we honor the process, we get resonance when we *arrive.*

From beginning to end, creativity isn't about speed—it's about depth.

> He has made everything beautiful in its time. He has also set eternity in the human heart; yet no one can fathom what God has done from beginning to end. (Eccl. 3:11 NIV)

How much more depth can we uncover over time?

One of my first books was written shortly after my decision to leave the church record label and ministry after accepting my role at the entertainment company. It was raw. It was honest. It was controversial. It was therapeutic in its own way. It was eye-opening and jaw-dropping. There was unfiltered beauty within the pages, but it would never see the light of day.

I couldn't fathom what Presence was doing during that season. I didn't recognize the margins. I didn't understand the power of waiting. I was in such a hurry to move forward that I never took time to let life breathe. My faith was challenged. There were seasons in my creative journey when I confused movement with maturity. If success didn't happen fast, I assumed something was wrong. When projects stalled or manuscripts were left in piles, creativity slammed against resistance. But the delay wasn't defeat: It was a lesson in the art of waiting.

> The least of you will become a thousand, the smallest a mighty nation. I am the LORD; in its time I will do this swiftly. (Isa. 60:22 NIV)

In the quiet, the margins took shape. I didn't understand it all at the time, but the slowdown was a setup. Those months in my buddy's office sorting through next steps, the early years of the creative house, the television series, the book deals, and the creative endeavors that developed. Each step of the way, Presence shaped not just the work, but me—my voice, my courage, my clarity.

Don't rush the reveal. Let creativity marinate. Let the vision steep. Let the voice mature. Let the fire refine you with depth until you're not just ready to be seen but ready to carry what Presence has been forming in you all along.

What I've learned through the art of the margins has been etched into my soul. It's who I am now and who I am becoming. It's where Presence is leading me. It's where my calling is stepping toward. It's where I find the edge of brave. But the reveal couldn't have happened without the steeping, maturing, refining, strengthening of courage to carry the weight in the hardest seasons.

For thirty years, I've been wandering in the wild chasing creativity. It's become a road map. It's become an unseen place where my faith has been tested and forged. It's also a place of warning if I'm tempted to stop digging ditches or drift from awe and wonder. It's been the oasis where I've learned to wait, where I've learned to listen, and where I've found depth in creativity.

The margins are often the safest place for raw ideas. They teach us to listen. They force us to deepen. They strengthen the unseen muscles of trust. And when the time is right, we'll step out with something that carries weight—not because we rushed it, but because we let it grow roots first. "I'm sure now I'll see God's goodness in the exuberant earth. Stay with GOD! Take heart. Don't quit. I'll say it again: Stay with GOD" (Ps. 27:13–14).

Take heart: The waiting isn't wasted. It's where the goodness of Presence strengthens us. Honor the process and stay rooted in the margins. Your creativity is being refined. Wait, and don't rush the reveal. When the time is right, He will reap a harvest. If you want your work to echo, trust Him and see what He will do.

29

BEAUTY IN BONFIRES

In the darkness of the wild, a beautiful bonfire blazed. Fiery orange and vibrant yellow, a magnificent glow shone bright as the sun. Around the bonfire were shadows across generations. Those from the past. Others from the present. Some were forgotten. Those who were close, and others who crossed my path through the seasons. Of course, Presence, Revelation, Creativity—the Rivers of Life—were there too. They'd always been. My gaze shifted knowing somehow each person influenced my journey, my craft, my calling.

Years of wandering in the margins forged my beliefs in wilderness seasons. A journey where I clung to the Rivers of Life when no one else was there. Seasons when I walked alongside wisdom givers and doubt killers who helped guide me through the wild. Along the path, I'd walked with those who shared their stories and their creativity with me. For some, their search in the margins was for fame, fortune, success, and survival. For others, the wild was one of purpose, passion, and revival in a broken world.

Not all were believers. Not all were followers. But most were fellow wanderers digging ditches of creativity. Digging. Planting. Searching. Seeking. Those who dug deep enough found greater purpose. Those who barely broke ground searched for stronger courage. All searched for the Rivers of Life in their own way.

I'm not a preacher. I'm not an evangelist. I'm a ditch digger.

In my brokenness and flaws, I've encountered moments when I've shared my calling, my craft, and my journey to be closer to the Rivers of Life. My name may never be in bright lights. My creativity may never pack stadiums. My calling may never gain the world's acclaim. But that's the essence of living in the art of the margins: All harvests will fade unless the Rivers of Life flow through me and my creativity draws fellow wanderers to do the same.

That's the beauty of bonfires: All are welcome.

Our testimonies are how we fight the darkness. Our truth shines the light of Presence in bonfires. Our courage draws us to Revelation as the beauty of revival influences culture. "To bestow on them a crown of beauty instead of ashes, the oil of joy instead of mourning, and a garment of praise instead of a spirit of despair" (Isa. 61:3b NIV).

We will encounter seasons alongside Creativity when we stand in the ashes, when we're broken in mourning, and when we drop to our knees in despair. But in the margins, the Rivers of Life show us another way. Around the bonfires, we find the beauty of inspiration, healing, courage, joy, worship, and community.

As I've shared before, one of the most influential voices in my life is my friend Mitch. He's one of the wisest people I know, and he's also one of the most biblically sound. Whenever I have questions, he goes straight to the Word. He's one of the reasons my faith has been sustained. His wisdom is rooted in more than the world's street smarts; it's rooted in the beauty of Scripture. I'm forever grateful for his brotherhood around the bonfire.

Around the bonfire is someone else whom I'd met a handful of times in seasons past: Greg Laurie. During my years in ministry, we partnered with Greg and Harvest Crusades. I remember sitting in a green room one night, invisible, like I'd been to most influential leaders. I was surprised when Greg and his wife, Cathe, took time to talk with me. It wasn't a big deal to anyone else in the room. I'm certain neither of them will remember the conversation, but they left an imprint on my soul. They noticed the unseen. And I've tried to do the same with others ever since.

In the wilderness seasons, there were times when I stepped back from the bonfire because life was hard and my faith was challenged. Each time, I called Mitch—then I'd watch a message from Greg. Two wisdom givers who'd never met each other spoke into my life in powerful, soul-giving, and beautiful ways. Both endured real life, real challenges, real breakthroughs. And both have remained around the bonfire through the darkest and brightest days of the wild.

You see, the beauty of bonfires interrupts the darkness. It resists despair. It declares not all is lost from the light. In the chaos and confusion, fellow wanderers gathered around the flames and spoke when words failed. Beauty—words, music, wisdom, presence—is warfare. Our souls are reminded that heaven still touches earth. We fight for more than the world's victories or culture's acclaim. We fight for our calling and for the calling of those gathered around the bonfire in the name of the Rivers of Life.

We may never know who will gather with us around the flames, who our calling and creativity will reach, or when we might encounter them in the wild. Maybe you've pictured those around the bonfire and recognized how they've influenced your life, your calling, your creativity. Maybe those around the flames aren't who you expected. Some might be known leaders, and others might be wanderers like Stella in Zambia, unknown to the masses. The Rivers of Life bring those we need around bonfires to encourage, to strengthen, to just be with us at the right time.

We don't need to preach to the choir, recite a trending message, sing a catchy hook, or gather with only those who are like-minded. We don't need to guard our bonfires as if no one else is allowed to join. In the margins, the beauty of bonfires leaves us in the raw, the vulnerable, the real, surrounded by wanderers who have impacted our lives and influenced our creativity. When we strip the facade away, we gain lasting wisdom from their journey in the wild.

As wanderers of Presence, our gifts, our talents, our art, our craft, and our leadership are given to us for a greater purpose. Around bonfires, the roots grow deeper and the rivers flow wider. Presence reveals His beauty in the battles of the creative life through those around us. We learn how the art of obedience in our calling equips us to fight in a war for souls. Our craft is a weapon of light, not a road to fame and fortune. Creativity goes beyond influence and leadership rooted in what we gain in this world from our calling. Instead, the beauty of bonfires inspires us to create in sacrifice and shine brilliance through the light of Presence.

In the margins, we are reminded that the beauty of someone else's story and calling is not convenience for our own gain. We begin to see beauty of bonfires as legacy—not a mirror of self-ambition but a reflection of eternal sacrifice. We learn so much seated around bonfires in the margins. The wild of this world and culture needs more bonfires to break free from the grip of isolation, and creativity is how we draw them in to be closer to Presence.

When we spend seasons around bonfires, we stop chasing the beauty of the flame and become keepers of it. "The fire must be kept burning on the altar continuously; it must not go out" (Lev. 6:13 NIV). As keepers of the flame, we are called to keep the fire burning always as a reminder of the holiness of Presence and our continual need to worship and revere the Rivers of Life. Worship and faithfulness are reflections in the fire of our journey in the margins. Bonfires are altars to Presence where we gather and remember. We share testimonies of our need to be wrapped in His beauty and to be keepers of His creativity.

> Summing it all up, friends, I'd say you'll do best by filling your minds and meditating on things true, noble, reputable, authentic, compelling, gracious—the best, not the worst; the beautiful, not the ugly; things to praise, not things to curse. Put into practice what you learned from me, what you heard and saw and realized. Do that, and God, who makes everything work together, will work you into his most excellent harmonies. (Phil. 4:8–9)

In the margins, we fill our creativity with a calling that is true, noble, reputable, authentic, compelling, and gracious. We surround ourselves with those who share the same passion whether they are believers, seekers, or fellow wanderers. When we gather and witness beauty in the dark and brilliance in the light, there is harmony. And when we share our creativity—our testimony—rooted in the Rivers of Life, there is power.

The beauty of bonfires inspires us to create beyond first sparks through long seasons of fiery obedience. Starting is a threshold; staying is a legacy. Anyone can chase a spark or start a fire, but we must be willing to be keepers and carriers of the flame into eternity. We are called to wield our weapons of creativity to fight against the dark and protect the light. That's where our heart, our calling, our craft burns for deeper truth rooted in the grace of Presence—that's our legacy.

> Therefore, since we are surrounded by such a huge crowd of witnesses to the life of faith, let us strip off every weight that slows us down, especially the sin that so easily trips us up. And let us run with endurance the race God has set before us. We do this by keeping our eyes on Jesus, the champion who initiates and perfects our faith. Because of the joy awaiting him, he endured the cross, disregarding its shame. Now he is seated in the place of honor beside God's throne. (Heb. 12:1–2 NLT)

For nearly six decades, Billy Graham preached the gospel across continents. When I was young, I, and hundreds of thousands, attended one of Billy's crusades during a major week-long event at Hong Kong Stadium. Tens of thousands gave their lives to Presence.[6] Decades later, when my calling brought me to building the indie record label, I read Billy's autobiography, *Just As I Am*. His journey and wisdom within those pages became a framework for ministering to culture years ahead of its time.

When I finished reading his book, it was clear to me that he guarded his fire with discipline, accountability, and prayer. His life reminded me to keep the fire lit by tending daily to the source of the flame. I'd like to believe he's been around my bonfire from time to time.

One of the most powerful messages Billy shared wasn't in a stadium in front of hundreds of thousands. It was filmed while he was seated in a weathered leather chair in his home. Nearing a century, he was more frail, his voice gravelly, yet his message and legacy remained strong as a rock.

> As I look back over my life, it's full of surprises. I never thought I would become friends with people in different countries all over the world. I see how God's hand guided me. When I began preaching many years ago, it was not with any thoughts that I'd be preaching to large audiences. God has done this.[7]

Around the bonfires, we gather in the margins from all walks of life. Our calling rooted in our unique gifts of creativity. We have all turned our back on Presence in the margins, through seasons in the wilderness, in the wild of this world. But we don't have to remain in those unseen places. Only one message will change the hearts and lives of culture for eternity. That is our common purpose around the bonfires; that is where we find Presence guiding us toward resurrection, restoration, and revival.

Revelation endured our shortfalls, our bloodstains, our failures so we can reflect the mighty love and faithfulness of Presence. We deserve ashes, brokenness, mourning, despair, and yet, as carriers of the light, the brilliance of bonfires offers us healing, courage, joy, worship, inspiration, and community. Presence sees Revelation in us, and there is freedom.

> For the message of the cross is foolishness to those who are perishing, but to us who are being saved it is the power of God. (1 Cor. 1:18 NIV)

As I've been writing the pages of this book, I've thought a lot about heaven. I've wondered what it will be like to walk in eternity alongside the Rivers of Life. My imagination flows to the most beautiful oasis, the most bountiful harvest, the crystal-clear rivers flowing and reflecting beauty, love, compassion, reverence, and worship. I've pictured wanderers around the bonfires: those I've lost, those I've never met, those who are still wandering with me. From the great heroes of the faith from Scripture to warriors in the fight forgotten by the world. And I've asked myself, "What is the legacy I hope to leave behind?"

In the margins, I'm convinced the Rivers of Life will keep guiding me to the answer found in a calling of eternity. Legacy is forged in the journey, the digging, the planting, the watering, the oasis, the bonfires, and the courage to create as we wander toward the edge of brave. We return to the work. We return to the why. We return to the altar. And we are not alone. We are gathered around beauty of a holy bonfire ablaze with faithfulness, obedience, resilience, community, Presence, Revelation, and Creativity. A flame that doesn't fuel itself from the world—because it's been lit by heaven.

30

MASTER THE MARGINS

Three days on the Zambezi shifted the course of my journey, my craft, and my calling as Presence invited me into the margins. With rooted authority, He guided me along an unexpected path toward the unseen in obscurity. He has walked with me in seasons of catching my breath, steadying what was shaken, healing what was broken, and searching for what was lost.

Presence has whisked me away in the margins toward awe, wonder, and bonfires. Through seasons of heaviness and freedom, a quiet rhythm of originality has echoed in the wild. Presence placed a blank page in front of me and whispered, "What will you do with this?"

The margins were an epic adventure waiting for me, but the journey was dangerous. No promises of certainty, only a call for courage. No flattering with predictability, only a forging of faith in a holy fire. The margins were wild with the unknown. Each step lured me beyond what was familiar to search for raging rivers beneath the soil. Presence promised to do His most profound work in me in the unseen places.

But I had to choose.

> For we are God's handiwork, created in Christ Jesus to do good works, which God prepared in advance for us to do. (Eph. 2:10 NIV)

Presence has prepared us in advance to do good works when we choose to embrace the art of the margins. The Zambezi became a threshold of my path toward the edge of brave—moments when Presence asked me to bury what had been and plant what could be. What I didn't understand then was the margins would become holy ground where Rivers of Life resurrected my calling, rekindled my creativity, and brought me to bonfires to learn and create with others.

When Presence asked me to stay amidst the uncertainty, I never imagined the margins in the wild would become an oasis where I dug ditches and planted seeds. It's become a catalyst, a commissioning, a grove of Joshua trees, and, at times, a battleground. Because "God's gifts and his call are irrevocable" (Rom. 11:29 NIV).

And now, after walking this journey with you through these pages, I'm compelled to invite you to create through the art of the margins too. This hasn't been my path alone. It's yours to plant in a creative oasis around the bonfires of your journey. Presence, Revelation, and Creativity will walk with you into the unknown ... Rivers of Life flowing beneath the soil.

It's your moment to step across the threshold into the margins and run free in the wild. This isn't the end of the story: It's the moment when you pick up a shovel and start digging. Everything that has brought you here—the waiting that felt wasted, the wandering that felt pointless, the whispers in the dark you weren't sure were from Presence—has all been preparation. Presence never simply hands us ideas; He hands us invitations.

Invitations to build. To speak. To create. To become.

The invitation is now. Are you courageous enough to accept it?

Maybe you've seen what happens in the margins. You've seen how Presence meets us in the places where no one else applauds. You've seen how creativity is forged in obscurity, how excellence is shaped in silence, how beauty emerges not from ease but from surrender. Maybe you've gathered around bonfires and heard stories of those who risked the yes, who kept the fire lit, who carried the flame, who created from the real and the raw and the holy.

If that's you, then keep digging ditches.

Keep going deeper. Keep creating. Keep being original.

I hope to see you one day around the fire.

For those who are weary in a wilderness season, find a bonfire and sit for a while. Then pick up a shovel and dig deep until you hear the river flow. Presence isn't finished with your story, your creativity, your calling. Chase the wonder beneath the soil, and experience where the river leads. There's no greater adventure than to create and return to awe in the wild.

For the fearful, weathered, or worn wanderer, this is a moment in the margins, in your creativity, in your calling, that requires bravery, not performance. Obedience, not applause. Surrender, not certainty. It requires courage that forges your calling in eternity in saying yes. For some, this might be for the first time, and for others, it might be the thousandth. For all, it means risking the yes again and again.

You weren't called to walk someone else's path. You weren't designed to mimic someone else's voice. You weren't created to shy away from fear in the wilderness. You were shaped by Presence, who paints possibilities in the sky and writes calling in obscurity. You were made to live in the wild. Your pain, your breakthroughs, your grit, your grace—all are part of the creativity He is crafting through your life in the margins. Culture needs more wanderers, more doubt killers, more of those willing to create from the real, the raw, the holy.

For some, creativity is painting. For others, it looks like writing, directing, producing, singing, or leading. Maybe it looks like building businesses, ministries, stories, strategies, solutions, teams, systems, spaces of healing, spaces of justice, or spaces of hope. But for all, it begins with a blank page. If you've been creating on the blank pages for a while, maybe it still looks like digging. Digging for clarity. Digging for courage. Digging for obedience. Digging for wonder. Digging and believing Presence is preparing a future that's not yet shaped.

Choose today to step across the threshold into the margins. The shovel is in your hands. The wild is calling. Your journey to the edge of brave is guided by the hands of Presence, Revelation, Creativity. The Rivers of Life aren't handing you a map; they're offering you deeply rooted faith to flow in your creativity. Faith that you will be forged in the reflection of Presence. You just have to be willing to dig deep enough.

Isaiah understood the shaping of Presence better than most: "In the same way that this potter works his clay, I work on you, people of Israel" (Jer. 18:6b).

Our lives are not just something *we're* shaping. Our lives are being shaped by Presence. Life itself becomes a masterpiece of Presence, and we become the living artwork He continues to mold, form, and forge with care. We are the workmanship of Presence, created to walk in the footsteps of Revelation to do good works—to create courageously. We are all called and gifted in ways that can't be revoked. But the art of the margins was never meant to be mastered alone.

We are not only called to create in the wild, we are called to champion the creativity of fellow wanderers around bonfires. The margins are full of artists who need encouragement, writers who need someone to read their words before anyone else, entrepreneurs who need someone to believe in their idea before it's viable, leaders who need to be affirmed so they will affirm others, ministries and organizations who need to be supported before they are celebrated.

Around the bonfires, we learn how creativity rooted in honor thrives in the margins. Our calling is multiplied as we dig deeper ditches, not only in our own oasis but in the oases of others. Our obedience in the wilderness becomes bonfires of testimony.

Remember, buried doesn't mean dead.

Every great movement—every culture-shifting, freedom-seeking revolution—begins not with one masterpiece but with many. Many voices. Many visions. Many brushstrokes. Many shovels breaking ground in the wild. The margins are holy ground where we stop competing and start cultivating. Where we rise and raise other wanderers with us. Where we celebrate what Presence is forming in others with the same joy and passion as what He is forming in us.

When we cross the threshold and begin our journey toward the edge of brave, we must fight for others in the margins. Champion their creativity. Call out their potential. Make room for their ideas around the bonfire. Cheer for their bravery. Protect their beginnings. Celebrate their steps in wilderness seasons. Honor their oases. Hold their testimonies with reverence. Believe in them until they believe in themselves. Allow others to borrow our courage until they discover their own. And pick up a shovel and dig a few more ditches for them.

If you've chosen to step over the threshold for the first time or the thousandth—welcome, and welcome back. The margins are not where your story ends; they are where your calling begins. They are where your creativity grows deep and wide. Obscurity is not punishment; it is preparation. Your creativity may be hidden, but Presence sees every ditch you dig and every seed you plant. He does His greatest work in the quiet of the wild so He can do His loudest work through surrendered wanderers.

Dig deep to the underground rivers of calling so your creativity will shift and shape culture. You'll discover the soil becomes unseen faithfulness where breakthroughs bring freedom. Your voice is forged for this moment. Return to awe with courage, and walk in wonder on holy ground as you master the art of the margins.

The blank page is in the hands of Presence. He is still shaping, still forming, still working the clay. The margins are wide and wild and waiting. The shovel is in your hands; unearth with each strike echoing of eternity. Go deeper in courage. Go deeper in discipline. Go deeper in obedience. Deeper in the wild to create, to encounter, to gather around bonfires. Then help fellow wanderers do the same. Because your story has only just begun.

The margins are calling. And a bonfire is still lit.

ACKNOWLEDGMENTS

To Presence, who walks with me in the wild: My creativity and calling remain rooted deep in You. To the wife: Your sacrifice, love, and support are unwavering and unmatched—our daily laughter continues to forge our adventure together. To Linda: Your relentless commitment to my creativity goes beyond this book as we've stood shoulder to shoulder in the fire. To the David C Cook team: Your unique creativity is expressed in every page to bring this dream and message to life. To Jeri: Your gifts continue to fuel the foundation of not only this book and movement but so many creatives around the bonfire. To Mitch: I'm so grateful and humbled that you've guided the story behind the stories in our brotherhood. To Marc: Your steadfastness in all of my creative endeavors inspires me to keep digging deeper. To those who have shared their stories within these pages: Your courage and relentlessness fuel the creativity of others. Keep digging. And to the reader: My prayer throughout these pages is to offer an invitation for you to become a ditch digger in the margins too.

To all who have wandered with me in the wild: Thank you.

NOTES

Chapter 2

1. "Blessed Assurance," by Fanny Crosby and Phoebe Knapp, published 1873, Public Domain, accessed April 11, 2026, https://hymnary.org/text/blessed_assurance_jesus_is_mine.

Chapter 5

2. D.J. Williams, *The Disillusioned* (Forgotten Stories, 2013).

Chapter 8

3. *The Chronicles of Narnia: The Voyage of the Dawn Treader*, directed by Michael Apted (20th Century Fox, 2010), film.

Chapter 13

4. *The Lord of the Rings: The Fellowship of the Ring*, directed by Peter Jackson (New Line Home Entertainment, 2002), extended ed. DVD.

Chapter 18

5. "2786. Képhas," *New American Standard Exhaustive Concordance of the Bible*, Bible Hub, accessed April 17, 2026, https://biblehub.com/greek/2786.htm.

Chapter 29

6. Danny Mok, "'Tens of Thousands' in Hong Kong Became Christians After American Evangelist Billy Graham's Rousing Gospel Rallies," Religion, *South China Morning Post*, February 23, 2018, www.scmp.com/news/hong-kong/community/article/2134349/hong-kong-remembers-american-evangelist-billy-graham-and.

7. "Billy Graham: 'Are You Ready to Die?'," posted by Billy Graham Evangelistic Association, February 21, 2022, www.youtube.com/watch?v=-Y7kULLmtL0.